CONTENTS

Contents

PREFACE

Starting a small business is similar to getting married—in the long term, a high percentage don't make it. But how can this happen? You've invested much of your capital resources and worked long hours; isn't that enough? Unfortunately, money and hard work *are not* enough. Start-up money will keep you going for a while, but eventually it runs out, and you'll get to a point at which you've reached your borrowing limit. Anyway, isn't the objective to take money out, not put it in? Long hours and hard work are admirable, but not always the secret to success. Running a business of your own is more mental than physical. Marketing and sales are part of the job whether you like it or not. You'll be ahead of the game if you know how to find people who get a lot of flat tyres, rather than simply rely on being the best at fixing them. Being streetwise will give you the advantage in today's competitive world.

This book will show you how to change your thinking and succeed at the things that will make your business survive and prosper. It will suggest ideas for serving and caring for your customers, so you won't have to lose sleep at night. It will suggest things *not* to do and how to rectify the situation if it's already too late. These are ideas that I've used throughout the years to keep a business open and operating when others would have just walked away. These ideas were learned the hard way—the *streetwise* way. Remember that suppliers and creditors don't want to see anyone go out of business; they just want to be paid. If there's a chance of your business surviving and getting back on its feet, they want to help. So don't run away and hide; if you ask for help and come up with a plan, many times you can work it out together. Being open and honest with creditors will give you the best chance to bounce back.

Some business owners will find themselves in a situation in which the bullets are coming from all directions at once. You'll discover ways to hold them back and give you breathing room, and to solve problems, in the following chapters. You'll discover ways to avoid problems and recognise and correct slumps. As long as your business is still open and you have customers, there's a good chance you'll make it. Many of the ideas are from personal experiences I've had in my businesses. But losing small battles is not always a bad thing if it can be a lesson you'll remember later down the road.

Sometimes there is too much damage already done, and the odds are stacked high against you. Don't put your head in the sand—stand up and face it head on. If you follow the proper procedures, you'll come out of it with fewer scars, and ready for a new challenge. I've even seen cases in which old suppliers and creditors will help you get started again. Knowing what you can do and being honest with creditors will be to your best advantage.

Now you may ask, "Why are you qualified to write this book?" In more than 30 years of owning and operating small businesses, I have been involved with or faced many of the things you will read here. More times than I can count, one of my businesses was faced with problems, including those of cash flow, which had to be solved for my business to survive. And if it didn't happen directly to me, I have seen many situations with friends' and customers' businesses. In a lot of instances, I will tell you what didn't work and what did. Believe me, being there and doing it makes a lasting impression. It's hard to forget the mistakes that were made and the sleepless nights worrying about where the next payment is coming from. I can still remember the headaches and the anxiety when answering the next phone call. Experience is a great teacher.

Even if your business is not on the brink of disaster, this book will show you ways to avoid pitfalls. You will find the first chapter to be the longest, because it's about the most important part of keeping a business thriving: taking good care of customers. Doing the opposite or being indifferent to a problem will lead to negative growth. Chapter

1 takes you through situations that should not happen; and you can check your business to see if they are happening. Being aware of what can happen *before* it happens will make it easier to overcome obstacles that will occur. Just like a serious medical condition, identifying problems early will give you the best chance of curing them before real disaster strikes. So, if you need help now, it's here. If you want to be prepared, just in case, the ideas are here for that as well. Learn how to keep your business moving toward the goals you set in the beginning. You'll find success hiding right behind those problems that you need to solve.

DISCLAIMER

Please note that not every proposed solution in this book will work for every business, and that you will need to decide for yourself whether your business is viable in the long run or not. If your business is unlikely to generate more income than it will incur in costs in future, it might not be wise to continue with it. This book is designed to help the many businesses that are viable in the long run.

It can be very risky to borrow money personally to lend to or invest in a struggling business and this book makes no claim as to whether or not that would be a sensible thing to do.

If your business continues to trade when you know you are unable to pay bills as they become due for payment then you might be found guilty of fraudulent trading which could incur personal liability.

If you have any doubts or questions about any of this please consult your accountant or a solicitor.

Crimson are publishing this book in good faith to try to help you, however we cannot accept any responsibility for decisions you take as a result of reading this book. You are solely responsible for any actions you take or decide not to take as a result of reading this book.

CHAPTER 1
Poor Customer Care

It all starts here—or ends here if you're not careful. It's obvious that if there are no customers to buy your products or services, there is no business. Why put your company in this undesirable position? It should never happen—and won't—if you pay attention to what's going on. You should have a plan or policy that *everyone* in your business is aware of. Customer care, a.k.a. customer service, is expected at a high level today, and if it's below that, repeat business can and will suffer. Business owners know how difficult it is to acquire new customers. You'll spend a lot of money on high-quality advertising, direct mail, discount prices, special sales, and free offers just to get them to call or shop at your store. Once you've got their attention, don't let them go by providing poor service and indifference.

The big companies have a term called Customer Relationship Management (CRM). They have meetings and classes for their middle management and employees to teach them the basics. Their problem (with a few exceptions) is that they don't practise what they preach. They don't reinforce the principles that make customers happy and satisfied. They treat everyone the same and expect all customers to follow the same buying procedures. Think about all your friends and relatives; can you find two that are the same? Can you think of two that want to do the same thing, the same way, at the same time? So how can you expect your customers to line up like a row of ducks following their mother? They will always be looking for a way to escape when the opportunity presents itself. And once they're gone, it's extremely difficult to get them back. You want customers to buy from you because *they* want to, not because *you* want them to. You must provide the personal service and a general atmosphere that reinforces their loyalty. Customers will only give their loyalty; you can't just take it or expect it.

Streetwise business owners know that great customer care shows that you really appreciate their business. It's the biggest defence you have against the large, national stores and major companies. They lure people into their businesses with massive advertising and ridiculously low prices. Once they've got the customer, they move them through their store like cattle going to slaughter. Who wants to be treated this way? Give the buying public and business customers an alternative. To stay in business and grow, you need your customers to come back, over and over again. Poor customer care will only put you in a box where the sides keep getting higher. After a while, you'll never get out and the word will spread. Look for ways to make buying from your business a pleasant experience, and you'll reap the rewards now and in the future. It all starts with the owners and the management; a business is not born with exceptional customer care, it's taught and learned. Be the teacher, not the preacher.

Never Never Land

Customer care is the foundation on which loyalty and positive word-of-mouth advertising are built. Especially during difficult economic times, losing *any* customers is not in your best interests. Many small business owners are not even aware that negative situations exist, because they fail to check on their front-line customer contact people regularly. Employees who work directly with your customers need to be trained, retrained, and reminded to avoid these situations. Remind your front-line people (and yourself) that the customer is really the one who pays the bills *and* their wages. Without them, what do you have?

Hold regular meetings, have literature available to reinforce customer care policies, and let employees bring up unusual customer situations that previously occurred. Discuss solutions together and decide the best approach for when it happens again. Make it compulsory that all of your employees attend these customer care meetings.

The following ideas are things you never want to happen in your business; watching for them in advance can prevent them from happening. If you wait too long and damage has occurred, it's much harder to reverse. Most of these *nevers* are easy to correct if you know that they are going on, so be observant and vigilant.

- *Never* forget to say thank-you after every sale or order. Don't assume you're doing a customer a favour by selling to them; you need them more than they need you. People may not notice every time you thank them, but they will remember if you don't. And it should be said in a sincere and honest manner.

- *Never* tell customers or clients that you will call them back at a certain time, and then fail to do it. Make the call even if you don't have all the information, and let them know you're still working on it. By not calling, you make them wonder if you forgot, or if their request is just not important enough. Even if it's not at the top of your to-do list, it may be significant to them, so don't let them down. Make the contact and keep them informed.

- *Never* let customers see employees standing around talking when they are waiting in line to make a purchase. I see this all the time in fast food restaurants and it makes me want to walk out. Train them to ask how they can help, and watch them periodically to see that they are doing it.

- *Never* promise anything that you can't or won't deliver. Your customers will expect what you promise them, and will not be satisfied with less. They won't be able to trust you in the future, which means no repeat business and no referrals. The policy should be to promise less and deliver more.

- *Never* ignore people who enter your store or place of business. Acknowledge their presence and let them know that you'll be with them shortly. They represent a potential sale that you don't want to lose. If they feel overlooked or unimportant and leave before being helped, you have lost both a sale and repeat business.

11

- *Never* leave people on hold for more than a minute without checking back with them. The time goes much more slowly when you're just waiting, and it can destroy a customer's attitude. A recording with music and brief information about your company can create a diversion that makes waiting easier. Your customers might even learn about other products and services you provide for additional business. Also, provide a way for them to leave a message if they get tired of waiting.

- *Never* set business hours that are convenient only for yourself and let customers go elsewhere if you're not available. Your goal should be to first serve the customers, not yourself. Be flexible and open for business when it's most convenient for your target market to buy. Trying to make customers conform to your scheduling is counterproductive, and will force them to use your competitors who may have more suitable hours. Also, don't lock the door in front of people trying to get in, even if it's closing time. Stay a little longer, welcome them, and be happy they're there. If you're still in your office after regular hours and the phone rings, answer it, and help the caller in any way you can.

- *Never* screen customer service calls—take them all promptly and professionally. Don't ask who is calling; no one likes to be interrogated before they can ask a question. Have knowledgeable people ready to take calls and answer inquiries during business hours. Helping customers and answering customer questions in a timely manner will build loyalty and confidence in your business. Putting customers or prospects through a hassle will only make them hesitant about a future purchase.

- *Never* let the phone ring more than four times before answering it. Some people won't wait, and others will be irritated, which is not the way to start off a business conversation. Answering on the second or third ring is preferred even if you must ask them politely to hold briefly. If you're very busy and just won't get to the call soon, ask for a phone number and call them back promptly. I hate it when I can't speak to at least one live person during normal business hours.

- *Never* allow front-line employees to be rude or discourteous. If they are having a bad day, send them home rather than risk losing a sale or a customer. A bad experience will remain in the customer's mind for a long time. If it happens often with the same employee, you need to consider replacing him or her or transferring him or her to a different job without customer contact. You just can't afford to let someone with a bad attitude destroy morale and alienate customers.

- *Never* delay in making a refund or exchange; do it quickly and with a professional and friendly attitude. If you have a guarantee or warranty, back it up completely, and as soon as possible. Delays create bad feelings and bad publicity. If the customer feels comfortable making a return, he or she is likely to buy from you again. If you are lucky, these customers will also convey their experiences to friends and associates. Create that comfort level and the feeling that they cannot lose by being your customer.

- *Never* ignore customer suggestions; rather, welcome them with an open mind. Customers see things from a different perspective and may offer great ideas for improving your business. If they are regular customers, let them know that you're reviewing their ideas. Offer some type of reward or acknowledgement for any suggestions that you use. Let your employees and other customers know where the idea came from, and encourage others to do the same. After all, they are telling you how to make them happier when purchasing your products and services. So have some type of customer suggestion box or special email address where they can easily communicate with you.

- *Never* make customers wait to pay for their purchases any longer than absolutely necessary. Once your customers make their selection, they want to finalise the purchase as soon as possible and go on to other things. Standing in line at a cash register or checkout is just wasted time that they get nothing for in return. The owner or manager should be on the lookout for these situations, and should be willing to jump in and help until things ease up. A few people may even walk away, and that's a lost sale that should never happen.

- *Never* drag your feet when solving a problem or handling a dissatisfied customer. Get the facts and offer a solution that you can live with, and, most importantly, that the customer is also happy with. Your customers are more likely to remember how quickly the situation was resolved and the owner's or employee's attitude before they remember the solution. When you solve the problem in a cordial and timely manner, many customers will establish a comfort level for future purchases. They will know that if anything happens in the future, you'll take care of it without a hassle. For larger problems, the owner(s) should get involved and offer to guarantee the solution.

- *Never* forget to reward regular customers and frequent buyers. Even little perks such as a small discount, or a little extra or faster service, can go a long way toward keeping them. Most customers want to know that you appreciate their business, and that they are not only cash in the register. Even remembering their favourite products, either mentally or in your computer, makes them feel important. Don't you feel good if you walk into a shop and they say, "The usual, Mr Wilson?" Find ways to personalise the sale.

- *Never* have a sale and not have enough products on hand to fill everyone's purchase. If it's a clearance sale, state how many items are available on a first-come first-served basis. Don't let customers rush to your shop or call your order department only to be disappointed. The next time you have a sale, it may be ignored, and the word of mouth will be negative. Set a short time period for your sale, and if you run out of popular items, at least run a limited time offer so people can still get the sale price when additional supply comes in.

- *Never* charge for top quality and substitute with poor quality. Your customers will eventually find out, and you'll be history. Your competitors would love to use this information to steal your customers away. Don't give them the opportunity just so you can make easy money. Fair profits and good quality will make you more money in the long run. Be known as the company that gives value equal to or exceeding the price.

- *Never* interrupt customers when they are talking. It's not only impolite, but it also doesn't give you the opportunity of picking up valuable information. When you interrupt, it gives the impression that you're not really listening to what they are saying. Let them finish their thoughts, and wait for a question at the end. They may be telling you how you can sell to them quickly, and what's most important to them.

- *Never* answer all incoming calls with voice mail. Your customers and prospects may have immediate needs and can't wait for a return call. They may just call your competitor who will have a real person answer and make the sale before you even get your messages. It can also make customers feel that you're screening all your calls and they're not good enough to get right through. Have someone available to answer your incoming calls with a friendly and helpful voice.

- *Never* underestimate the value of a repeat order and the lifetime value of a customer. The lifetime value is usually based on what a customer spends in one year, times 20. Go ahead, work it out, and you'll probably be surprised at how big the number is (and this is only one customer). Do this for all your regular customers and add the totals together. You'll soon realise why you don't want to lose even one regular buyer. They are what builds your business and helps you survive during tough economic times. It makes you understand why one order or purchase is not worth losing a customer.

- *Never* chew gum or eat anything when talking to a customer on the phone or in person. It's disrespectful and shows that you put your needs ahead of theirs. Chewing gum is usually a nervous habit that you don't want to convey to someone who is relying on you for important information. It's just a common courtesy to give your full attention to your prospect without any background noises. If you could see yourself on a video eating or chewing, you'd be surprised at how improper it looks. It doesn't matter if you have a fast-food restaurant or a financial firm, proper etiquette is important.

- *Never* forget to ask for referrals or letters of reference. Most customers won't offer them unless you ask, and they can help build your business quickly. There are two types of referrals: The first one is a person who calls you and says they know your customer. The second is a name of a person given to you whom you must call or visit. Follow up without delay, and be sure to name drop the person who referred him or her. When times are tough, contact old customers and start this process. Remember, the price of a phone call is a lot less expensive than an advertisement that isn't working. Referrals are out there, so ask.

- *Never* be a small business owner that's too busy to talk to prospects and customers. Many people will buy from a smaller shop or company because they *can* talk to the top people. Be available and let customers know you're there if they need you. A short, handwritten thank-you note from the owner to a new customer will be long remembered. They will know that you're aware of their purchase, and that their business is appreciated. And we all like to spend our money where we feel the owner doesn't take us for granted. So, be visible and available whenever possible.

- *Never* make customers or prospects wait more than 24 hours for quotes, estimates, or special order information. Offer an estimated figure right away if you can, and then promptly supply the exact proposal. Show that you're eager to get their business or start their order. It will also give them the feeling that their order or purchase will be handled without delay. You don't want to give the perception that they will have to keep checking back with you for progress on their order. If you want their business, go get it before they start checking elsewhere.

- *Never* treat all customers the same, because they're not. Some need more attention than others to make a purchase. Others want to be left alone to make their own decisions, and will let you know when they are ready. Try to figure out who wants help right away, but make sure you are still available to others. You'll also find that some customers need a little reassurance that they are doing the smart thing by buying now. Another type will know that they want and desire to purchase it quickly and get out of the shop or off the phone; don't slow them down with needless chit-chat. Adjust to each personality type or buying habit and you'll have happy repeat customers.

- *Never* close your shop, office, or factory just so you can go on holiday. Have a well-trained employee take over with a way to contact you for any big decisions. If there's a slow season in your type of business, encourage employees to take time off or use their holiday time then. No more than 25 percent should be gone at any one time. If you just close up and disappear for a week or two, your customers may do the same and run to your competitors. If they are ready to buy and you aren't available, someone else will get their business. Holidays are great, but business comes first.

- *Never* forget about customers that you haven't heard from for a while. Contact them and see what's going on. In a business account, the buying contact person may have changed, and the new person may not know about you or can't find past information. Consumers will also tend to drift away and not remember your business; they may have misplaced your information or phone number, so remind them. Don't wait until it's too late—have a plan in place to contact old customers. If it's been a while since their last purchase, get on the phone or send them a reminder in the mail.

- *Never* try to fool a customer or the joke will be on you. People are smarter than you think, and even if they don't say anything, you'll probably never see them again. Be honest with your customers and give them more than they expect. Saying one thing and doing another will quickly destroy loyalty and word-of-mouth advertising. You want your customers to be your allies, not your adversaries. Give them value that they feel they are paying for, and keep them informed.

Bringing Them Back

Taking care of your customers now will mean that they'll be back when times are slow and new business declines. When your business starts hitting the bumpy road, run to your regular customers and hold on tight. At this time, worry less about profits and more about purchases and cash flow. I'll show you in later chapters how to use this cash flow to keep your business open and operating. Your valuable regular customers will still need to make purchases, and you don't want competitors or other desperate rivals to lure them away with ridiculous price offers. When they enjoy doing business with you and reach a comfort level, price becomes secondary. You can certainly see this in the motor trade where there would be no expensive models if people only wanted the cheapest transportation. Price only becomes a consideration when you have nothing else to offer.

You must also make sure that all your employees are on the same page as you concerning customer care. Doing the minimum is not good customer care. They must understand and believe in serving and assisting all patrons to give them the feeling they are a vital part of your business. Remind employees that without satisfied and repeat customers, no one has a guaranteed job. This is especially important during tough times, and should be augmented to include everyone in your company. As a business owner, you should realise how difficult it can be to acquire new customers, so don't let anything or anyone drive them away. If you have employees that don't seem to *get this*, they are probably not going to help your business survive when things get difficult. It's better to replace them before too much damage is done. Don't wait and make excuses to yourself; when you see the signs, act early. You can explain the situation and reasons to your other

18

employees after the problem person has left. Hopefully, they will understand that you are serious about customer care, and you won't accept less than their best effort.

By eliminating all or most of the *nevers*, you will have the best possible defence against your national competitors. People will remember how they were treated and how helpful you and your staff were. They know they won't get that at the big price discounters. But an unpleasant experience will quickly travel to their friends and associates. You want positive comments that convert to positive referrals. Don't take a chance on losing business before you even get it. Get to work today and get rid of those *nevers* that can only have a serious negative effect on your business.

Breaking Promises

One way to alienate customers and lose valuable trust is to say you'll do something, and then not do it. It doesn't matter whether you intended to do it and forgot, or just promised something to get a sale. Customers who have had this experience with your business will not forget it, and will lose faith in everything else you say or advertise. Why should they believe you? You've already demonstrated that you can't be trusted. About half of them will probably transfer their patronage to one of your competitors whom they think can be trusted. This lost business will multiply if you keep breaking promises and frustrating customers.

How would you feel if a friend says they will meet you at a restaurant at 7 p.m. and they're still not there at 7:30 p.m.? Or the car dealer service department says your car will be ready at 3 p.m. and the total cost is only £89? You show up at 3 p.m. only to find out it won't be ready until 6 p.m. and now it's going to cost £265! You buy a health insurance policy that's supposed to cover everything, and your first claim is rejected because of a preexisting condition. Get the picture? Doesn't it make you want to run from that business as soon as you can? This type of situation happens every day, and businesses do suffer lost customers because of it.

Customers will look at the promises you make as a test of your integrity and honesty. Passing that test will reinforce their loyalty and put them more at ease in the future. They will begin to feel comfortable doing business with you, and it will be very difficult for competitors to steal them away. But failing the test will result in just the opposite. They will wonder if they can ever believe anything you or your employees tell them. They will look at your products and your advertising, and question whether you can be trusted. And don't think that you can only lose one customer because of broken promises. Negative word of mouth travels much faster than positive word of mouth. Not doing what you say will also lose you prospects that hear negative word of mouth. And if it happens often, your business will develop a reputation that turns people away.

Reclaim Lost Customers

One of the best sources of new business can be old business. Those lost customers who no longer help fill your bank account are out there, and may even be waiting for you to come and get them, so don't disappoint them. Because they are previous customers, they know your company, but something changed at your business or in the market to make them leave. Maybe the person responsible for the negative situation is no longer there, and his or her replacement will be more receptive.

What do you do when you lose a customer? How long does it take to find out that you even lost him or her? If it's been long enough for him or her to buy from your competitors several times, you're definitely not keeping in contact with them often enough. The good news is, many lost customers can be won back if you make the effort; so don't pass up this extra revenue and profit—go after them. Unless there was an ugly argument that drove them away, they should be willing to talk to you or your company rep. Get over there and make a sincere effort.

The first step in reclaiming lost customers is to find out why they left in the first place. Some of the more common reasons are:

- A problem was not resolved.
- They moved out of your selling area.
- They no longer use what you sell.
- They are unhappy with your product or service.
- They found lower prices and higher value elsewhere.
- They had a past dispute with your company.
- There is a better selection at your competitor.
- They don't feel their business is appreciated.

- They had an argument with your sales rep.
- Technology left your company behind.
- A competitor stole them away.
- They now have a relative in the business.
- They went shopping for other sources.
- Delivery was late too often.
- Their business was closed or sold.
- They can't afford to purchase.

If you don't know why you lost them, ask and you will most likely get the answer. If they have moved out of your selling area and you can no longer provide them with products or services, it's probably a dead end. But if they were satisfied with your company, it's a good time to ask for referrals of potential customers they knew before they moved. Most people will discuss their reason with you, and you can use that information to avoid similar situations with other customers.

If you lost a customer due to an argument, no matter who won, it needs some time to rest. It may never be forgotten, but it can be forgiven and business can go on. Your initial approach should be cautious and not too presumptuous. A note, small gift, or new product literature can be a starting point to break the ice. Let that settle for a short time before making the first personal contact. Don't push too hard for more business, just let them know you're there and ready if they need you, and then make periodic follow-up contacts. Time heals, but don't avoid the situation completely, or you may never hear from them again.

With other lost customers, just ask what you can do to win their business back. When they tell you, pay close attention and come up with a solution or idea that satisfies their needs. Keep a record of what was agreed upon, and be sure that you and your employees follow through. If you disappoint your customer at this point, you will probably lose them forever. Let your staff know how this customer needs to be handled, especially if it's different from your normal routine. Your customer will expect you to keep your staff informed of any special arrangements agreed upon. You may even want to deal with them directly rather than with one of your staff members.

Lost customers are great prospects to help you grow, save, and rebuild your business. They already know you and your business, and were satisfied at one time. You also know about them from past transactions, which can help you serve them better in the future. Pursuing an old customer can be a challenging adventure with a positive result and feeling of accomplishment. And isn't it a good feeling to reclaim an old customer, especially from a competitor? Never write them off completely.

The Importance of Innovation and Improvement

A great way to keep your business going in a positive direction is to always offer new or improved products and services. Once you've defined your little corner of your target market, be on the lookout for needs and wants that aren't being met. In many cases, a little change or improvement on a current product can fill the need, and give you exclusivity, at least for a short period of time. Most new products and innovations are really updates or a better way of fulfilling a need. Even small changes can make a big difference. That's why computer software and operating systems keep offering new versions. The software companies' people know if they didn't offer it, someone else would. You need to be one step ahead of the crowd in your niche target market, and staying ahead will keep you out of trouble when the economy and market gets tough. Trying to catch up later and match a competitor can be a difficult, if not impossible, task. Be an innovator, not an imitator.

And while we're talking about competitors, when was the last time you shopped with them or visited their websites? If it wasn't within the last 60 days, do it soon. You don't want to be surprised and wonder why you're not getting any new business. Find out what they're doing right, and then find out what they're doing wrong, and advertise your company as a better alternative. You can't stop doing this, because your competitors are also finding ways of outdoing you. If they have a mailing list, get on it or have mail sent to a relative if the company knows you. If it is part of a big corporation, buy at least one share of its stock and you'll receive all its reports. When business gets tight, you want to get the bigger share. You want to trap your customers mentally, so there will be no question of where they should purchase.

Fighting for customers in a tight market is like 10 fishermen trying to catch five fish. You need the right equipment, the right fishing style, and the right bait. People are going to buy from somewhere, and it

22

might as well be from you. Once you catch them, you don't want to let them get away and be caught by someone else.

Don't Get Too Comfortable

Even when business is good and success seems simple, work on your customer care policies. Remember that even if you're at the top of your niche target market, your competitors are thinking of ways to knock you off. There's an old saying, "When you're at the top of your profession, the only way to go is down." And I can still hear Jackie Gleason saying "Be nice to the people you meet on the way up because you're gonna meet the same people on the way down." This is so true because most business owners have a goal of being on top. If that's where *you* are, you're the target for others. And don't think that because you haven't heard anything from them lately that they've forgotten about you. A general preparing for battle doesn't unveil his plan; he waits to make a surprise attack. So if you haven't experienced tough times yet, be prepared so they don't sneak up on you. Your competitors are planning ways to take your customers, sales, and profits. Don't be caught with your defences down! Have your plan ready and don't panic; it's part of the normal business cycle. Just about everyone who has a successful business went through difficult times and survived. Once you have made it past a trying period in your business, you'll be more prepared and wiser when the next one comes along.

CHAPTER 2
Insufficient Marketing

We've all heard the expression "too little, too late", but how many of us apply it to our business? Well, we hope it's not too late, but not using all the marketing tools available can put you in a hole that is hard to get out of. When you first open your business or buy an existing one, you usually have a gung-ho attitude toward promoting it. You try everything to find out what works while sales and market share is increasing. Throughout a period of time, you find what methods and venues work best for you and cut back on the ones that don't. You begin to use your marketing budget wisely and hone in on your valuable targets. A good marketing mix of advertising, direct mail, publicity, telemarketing, and other promotions will build a healthy business.

But what happens when your business is going well? Do you cut back on marketing because you don't want to spend the money or time anymore? Maybe you're thinking that everyone in your target market has seen your ads and received your mail. You've called everyone once or twice and the media won't run the same old press releases anymore. Thinking up promotions is too time-consuming when you would rather be playing golf. So you back off and put marketing on the back burner for a while. Then *a while* becomes permanent and you're not getting as many new customers as you once were. The results of this mistake will slowly creep up on you.

You begin to notice that your customer base is shrinking, and all of a sudden, sales are flat. You're losing customers due to normal situations such as moving, and your competitors are also stealing a few. Where are all the new customers that always found you and started purchasing? You can answer that question with another question: Where is all the marketing that brought you the precious new patrons in the past? If you cut back or stopped doing it, the answers are easy.

If you became too comfortable with your sales and target market share, you may have made the mistake of cutting way back on marketing. I say *mistake* because you can't turn the clock back; you'll need to almost start over again and rebuild your market awareness. Being present in front of your customers and prospects will get them to remember you through time. Even a casual presence (and not all of it costs money) will put a little icon in their mind. But it needs to be refreshed occasionally or it fades away. Whenever the need or want for your products or services arise, you want them to click on that icon and come knocking on your door or ringing your phone. Don't let too much time pass without some visible appearance in your target market. Let's look at five areas that can hold your business back and start you on a decline.

Too Little Advertising

Keeping your business name, logo, and product mix in front of your customers is essential to keep your company healthy and growing. Take it away and you lose the opportunity to acquire those new prospects that come along when you least expect them. New customers will become aware of your business only if they can find it or randomly see your advertising. But if your advertising is not *somewhere*, they will pass you by. You may be the best source for their needs, but how will they ever know if they can't find you? Casual customers who have purchased from you in the past will forget in time and need to be reminded. If you're not there to remind them, then someone else will be. Keep some advertising presence at all times, especially in the difficult times. When your business is slow, you don't want to lose *any* customers—they're just too valuable. If your competitors have stopped advertising or are close to going out of business, you can pick up new customers that are looking for a new place to buy.

This may not be the time to experiment and take new risks with advertising venues that haven't already proven themselves valuable. Stick with the tried and tested ways that have paid off in the past. If you have kept good records of past advertising performance, you'll know where to spend that limited budget. Don't spend money on advertising where you're unsure of the results. If you can't afford very much, start with the best and look for any discounts and deals available. Most of the time, you won't be offered a special discount if you don't ask. Talk to someone who can make a decision and tell him or her that you're on a very tight budget. Ask him or her, "What can you do for me with the limited money I have to spend?" If you have used him or her in the past, he or she probably values your business and will try to help you. He or she should realise that if he or she works with you now, you'll have some loyalty when conditions improve and you have more money to spend. If he or she doesn't realise it, tell him or her, and be very serious about it. You need people on your team that care about your business now *and* in the future. Too many compromises and the advertising company's salespeople see only the money and forget about tomorrow. If they don't help you today, all the tomorrows will be uncertain. Don't waste your time and money with those that are indifferent unless you absolutely have to.

Let's look at and consider some ways and methods of advertising that will help you acquire new customers and keep your current customers from forgetting you:

- *Trade publications*—They go directly to your target market and will be the first place prospects look when they need a new supplier or a new product. Having some presence in them should be a top choice if you can afford it.
- *Niche publications*—They reach a specific market such as small business, women, sports, and so on. When you're not only selling to a specific industry but a broader group as well, these can help. Check the magazine directory in your library to find them.
- *Daily paid-for newspapers*—In a large metropolitan area, these can be expensive. If you feel you must be in them, pick the best day or days and eliminate the rest to conserve capital.
- *Weekly paid-for newspapers*—Less expensive than the dailies and read by a majority of consumers. They usually highlight community news, schools and activities, so it's a good place if your products are for kids and families.

- *Free newspapers*—Usually weekly, and you can get some good exposure with consumers at a reasonable rate. At the lower end of the market, these are often black and white or one other colour. The major retailers often use the daily papers for their ads or inserts so won't drown you out.

- *National magazines*—Normally monthly, these are the top end of the ad market. They are all loaded with ads that cost a small fortune. Can you really afford to be in them, and will anyone even find your small ad? One way to save on expensive national magazine ads is to get on their list for last-minute ad space. Have your ads ready and save 50 percent or more. You may be able to write and submit a free article and get your contact information in the byline.

- *Radio*—If you sell to a local market, this can be an effective way of reaching your target audience. Check the cost for different times of the day and decide which will work best for you.

- *Cable/Digital TV*—If you have the budget and can visually demonstrate your products or service, this can be a great marketing tool. But because it's more expensive than other advertising, be sure you're getting a return that is proportionate to your cost. Good timing of your commercial can be the key to success. Short or long infomercial time may also be a fair choice. Ad costs can vary based on the number of viewers and time of day.

- *Phone directories*—National directories such as the yellow pages, Thomson and the phone book can be valuable, but also expensive. If there's only one in your area, you're lucky—use it wisely. In some areas there's a smaller, locally focused services directory, and these can be good as you're likely to get more ad space and hence more coverage.

- *Coupon books/flyers*—People love coupons, especially during tough economic times. Discounts don't have to be ridiculous, just a better-than-normal price. Always have a deadline for when the coupon expires, but make it long enough so they can use it at their leisure. Rather than mailing or printing all of them yourself, join a group book or flyer and let someone else distribute them. Just be sure it's going to your target market.

- *Websites*—Having your own website a few years ago was very expensive, but now everyone can afford it. Try offering printable coupons and weekly/monthly specials to entice prospects to visit often. Keep adding or changing things so that customers enjoy frequent visits.

- *Internet banners*—Being present on the internet today is important, if not essential. But the biggest problem seems to be getting people to visit your site, considering there are billions out there. Find sites that target the same market you do (but not competitively), and exchange banner links. If they are not interested in trading space, offer to pay a monthly fee if it's a great site.

- *Billboards*—Outdoor advertising can be used by both consumer and B-to-B companies for added exposure. Some of the best locations are near traffic lights or in an open area on a major road. Sides of buildings and bus stops can also work well if they attract the type of customer you're looking for. Call the number at the bottom of a billboard and see what's available.

- *Labels on products*—Offer other products or a discount on their next purchase or order by attaching it to a current product. Labels can be used anywhere to promote your company name or brand. Find other noncompetitive businesses and put labels/ads on each other's packaging or boxes. As long as you're selling to the same market, it can be an advantage to both businesses.

- *Buses and taxis*—For a shop, restaurant, or other local business, these signs can remind customers who you are and how to contact you. If you're a restaurant or bar, can you trade advertising with a taxi service to save cash? Don't cram too much into your message—name, slogan, one-line description, and contact information should be all you need.

- *Literature racks*—Small plastic racks can be purchased cheaply at a stationers. Offer to exchange with other

stores or offices and check on them regularly to be sure they are refilled. A good place to find other owners is a chamber of commerce meeting, where everyone is looking for new ideas.

- *In-store displays*—You can probably get a lot of these free from suppliers and distributors if you tell them you want to promote their products. You may even get a representative to give a live demonstration in your store. Nothing helps sales like seeing the product or service in use before they buy.

- *Promotional products*—Another inexpensive way to keep your name in front of customers and remind them of your products is through giveaways. If you select the correct items, customers will save them and use them. Your name will be ever present when they need to buy again. Try to give something that relates to your type of business.

- *Buyer's guides*—A lot of trade magazines in your industry will issue once-a-year buyer's guides that are distributed free to subscribers. A majority of them will offer listings in your specific category at no charge. Don't pass this up—no charge means that *anything* you get out of it puts you ahead of the game. Some professional associations also print buyer's guides, so be on the lookout for all of them.

The point I'm trying to get across is, *don't* stop all advertising when times get tough. Use what money you have wisely, and grab all the free stuff you can. Hiding under a rock and not spending anything is asking for more problems. What if no one lifts that rock? Where does that leave you, with slowing sales and no new customers? Sounds like the equation for disaster (and it is). Find some money somewhere and put it to good use.

Not Enough Direct Mail

I'm a big believer in direct mail, because it helped me save several companies when sales were decreasing. Somehow, I always found a way to keep sending those flyers, brochures, and samples to prospects. There were a couple of times I used the last cash we had available to

do a mailing to our best prospects, and it paid off. The orders we received more than paid for the mailing, and it helped us acquire new customers and repeat business. When you're tight on funds but want to keep mailing, here are a few things to keep in mind.

The List

You should have your own in-house list of customers and likely prospects. If you haven't mailed to current and past customers lately, that should be your first choice now. It will give you the best chance for quick orders and new business. There's an old adage that says, "Your current customers are your best prospects", and it's true. Just don't let them forget you; remind them periodically with literature, coupons, and anything else that is new and different. If you have a lot of different customers, divide them into two lists: A and B. The A list will be the shorter one with the customers who order often and more than others. The B list can include all others, such as casual customers and those who don't spend as much. When you need orders and cash flow fast, use the A list and make offers to entice buying now. Reminder postcards are another method that can encourage them to check current stock to see if they need to re-order. If using other outside lists, select the one that you've had the most response from in the past. Don't use the cost of the list as the criterion for mailing it. Orders and responses should be the reason you purchase it. When your budget is tight, it may not be the best time to experiment with new lists, regardless of the cost. Remember these new lists when conditions improve, and mail them; there may be a good prospect out there, but you just can't take the chance with limited funds. You want the highest probability of success now, so use the reliable list. It's the results that matter.

The Offer

If you want orders fast, then your direct mail offer needs to be a little better than previous ones. Try to appeal to buyers where they find it difficult to refuse. Whether it's price, delivery, upgrades, or added features, be willing to give more if they act quickly. Don't try to make giant profits and solve all your problems too quickly. It's better to get many orders with less profit to increase cash flow. Increased cash flow can help on a temporary basis by allowing you to pay some of your oldest bills.

Check old purchasing records to see your most popular products and services. Then make your direct mail offer with these as the leaders. Don't try to push old or obsolete items when you need to increase cash flow now. Save those for a clearance sale later when things settle down. If you have 10 popular products, make great deals on half of them in your mailing. You can then hope customers will add other products to their order at close to regular price. Supermarkets do this all the time, and there's no reason why you can't do it in direct mail. What you include in your offer must be something the prospect values to be effective. Be irresistible but not desperate.

Creating a Sense of Urgency

When a business needs orders and cash flow quickly, urgency becomes a factor. But what if your customers are not ready to buy or have enough of your product on hand? Why should they buy now and relinquish some of their capital? You must overcome these questions and roadblocks in their minds to entice them to act now. If your offer is good enough, there needs to be a deadline of when the offer will be withdrawn. You could also offer a bonus, free gift, upgrade or extra product (20 percent more, and so on) to order or buy now. Make it easy for them to order quickly by using a prepaid envelope, free phone number, fax, or the internet. You might even consider longer opening hours during the few weeks following the mailing.

If you use an external marketing firm, you can probably have 24/7 hours for receiving orders. The only setback is that some of your profits and cash flow will have to go toward paying the firm. But if you're doing a large mailing and don't have enough employees, or don't want to pay them for extended hours, an external marketing firm is the way to go. You want to create the urgency for customers to purchase quickly, and be available when they do. Take their money as soon as they are willing to spend it. When you really need cash in 30 to 45 days, set your deadline accordingly. *Buy Now* becomes the most important concern.

Getting Paid the Easy Way

Getting paid is the name of the game. Actually, there is no sale without payment. You want to offer as many payment options as you can. What's the difference how you get the money as long as you get it?

Almost any business can accept credit cards, and the two most common are Visa and MasterCard. If you only accept those two, you'll satisfy most of your customers. If you don't already accept them, contact your bank and ask to talk to the person who handles merchant accounts. Someone will be out to see you within 24 hours and have you set up with a processing machine in seven days or less. Once a charge is approved, the money will be in your account in 24 to 36 hours (except American Express, which takes a little longer). That's faster than a cheque clears, and it only costs you between 1 and 2 percent for the processing fee; it's worth it to have the money available. Credit card machines will also accept debit cards with a Visa or MasterCard logo on them. But not all merchant service providers are good for small business, and some are a rip-off. Read the contract carefully, and maybe even let your accountant look at it. Don't get caught in a situation that's difficult to get out of.

You can also offer extended payments with a deposit payment. Check with finance companies in your area to see if you can sell these extended payment contracts, and you will receive your money now (minus their fee, of course). If you accept cheques, there are many cheque guarantee services that will collect any unpaid or returned cheques. People want to pay in different ways, and the more options you offer, the easier it will be for them.

Too Little Publicity

Have you given up on getting publicity because you've had little luck in the past? Right now you're too busy chasing all your other problems and have no time to spend on something that's not a sure thing. Many business owners feel this way and think only the big companies get free publicity because they have more power and influence. This is NOT the general case; you can also get exposure in the media if you're creative and persistent. I said be *persistent*, not a *pest*. There is a difference, of course, and you don't want to be known as a pest. Being persistent means pursuing your goal in the face of rejection and opposition. Find the time to submit *newsworthy* stories and articles to the media where you will receive the most benefit. Try a different approach than you have used in the past. Look at your press release or story from the reader's perspective. Would you want to read this article or story? Ask others in your company to give their opinion, and make adjustments as needed. Here are a few ideas for obtaining free publicity when you need it most:

- Know the needs and editorial policies of the media; most have listings in directories at your local library.

- Find the name of the editor or reporter that can best assist you in your story or press release. Most of these names will also be listed in the media directories.

- When you find out what their deadlines are, fax or email your information just prior to when the paper is going to bed. If there is space that's unfilled, you may have a good chance of getting in. You won't know if you don't try.

- If a reporter or editor calls with additional questions, you must assume you're being taped. Everything you say should be honest and truthful because it will be on the record.

- Follow up with a phone call or email to see if your material is being used, and inquire if they need more information. If they don't remember what you sent, offer to resend it again immediately.

- Include any photos or graphics you can to catch attention. Most will not be returned, so don't send the originals. Offer more if you have them available.

- If your information and story concerns a national audience, try sending to wire services and news services. You'll also find these in the media directories at your library reference department.

- Request a copy of the publication and check it carefully to be sure all the information is accurate and correct. If it's a radio story, ask when it's being aired and listen carefully. If you find something you didn't say or are misquoted, request that they issue a correction.

- Submit all articles and stories on white paper with one-and-a-half or double-spaced copy. Don't use letterhead or coloured paper—it's distracting and not generally accepted in the industry. But don't forget to include your contact information.

- If your press release or story links to *breaking news*, send all materials special delivery. When the news is over, it's over, and you don't want to miss it.

- Last, and most important, don't submit anything that even hints at being an advertisement. You must convey your message in such a way that you interest or inform readers or listeners. Find a way to make your story newsworthy and you'll have a much better chance of your information being used.

Pursuing publicity can help greatly when your business is having other problems. It will give you free exposure in your target market at a time when you may have little money to spend. You shouldn't rely on it though; it's a hit or miss proposition, and it's hard to know when you'll receive it. But it's great when it works and should be a part of your marketing mix.

Too Little Telemarketing

I'm not talking about the kind of external telemarketing that takes your orders and calls: this is the section of your business you can expand or contract with the amount of business you are currently receiving. This type of customer care needs to be sufficient to provide the quality customer service that brings repeat orders. Make sure the group is doing an efficient job.

But the area where you can't just shut down and forget about it is your own telemarketing; almost every business does this to some extent. Whether it's calling to set up sales appointments, follow-up to direct mailings, or making an outright sale, telemarketing is necessary. When the time comes that you just can't afford to pay all your telesales team because results are few and far between, you will need to make adjustments. You know who your best sellers are; if not, look back at their results. Consider reducing your staff by 20 to 50 percent, and keep the best ones. This is no time to experiment with new employees or trainers; you need results, now. But don't stop making calls when funds are tight—just scale back a little until things pick up.

If you're using an outside telemarketing firm, have a meeting and discuss how you can reduce your costs by 30 to 50 percent and still get the service you need. If the firm can't come up with a workable plan, look elsewhere. There are great telemarketing firms everywhere, and some will value your business more than others. The one that helps you through the tough times should be the one you are loyal to when conditions improve. Remember, you can use a firm anywhere in the country for outbound calls; not only those in your town. Search around on the internet and compare. You don't want a company that's so large that you're only another number to them. Hire one that's small to medium size and really needs your business. They will do a better job and produce good results at a fair price. Dangle the carrot by telling them you'll increase your use of their services when things improve if they help you now.

If you're using a script for outgoing calls, take a hard look at it and consider some revisions. You need sales and orders now, so put some incentives in the presentation to generate a faster positive response. If using an outside firm, they may have a copywriter who can work with you to choose the correct words. Some things that can produce sales faster are:

- A discounted price with a deadline to buy. Don't make your deadline so far in the future that it will lose its effectiveness. You need sales this week, not next month.

- A special bonus or gift if they order or buy now, during the first call. It's worth giving something away because you save the time and cost of a follow-up call. Plus, no record-keeping and reminders to call back.

- Supply is limited, and when it's gone, the special offer is over. The old phrase "while supplies last" still works, and if they want it, now is the time for action.

- Free delivery or shipping if they buy now. Another incentive is free assembly if it applies. Most people hate to buy a product and then spend two hours putting it together.

- Buy now, pay later will work with some people. Although you need cash, the next best thing is an order placed. As long as you're 99 percent sure you'll get paid, an outstanding invoice or contract will look good on your balance sheet. You may even be able to borrow against it.

- A small discount or free delivery if they order and pay now with a credit card. The card fee is worth it if the money is in your account the next day.

- Offer to hold the price for additional purchases for up to six months or a year. This takes the doubt out of future orders and can allow customers to set an exact budget. Have an "order-by date" to get this offer and base it on payment within terms. This will give you immediate cash flow and the assurance of more orders in the future.

- Make follow-up calls shortly after the sale to ask if they are satisfied and have another offer to present. It's also a good time to offer add-ons and accessories for additional sales. Find the time and money to do some telemarketing in order to gain sales, which are so important when business is slow. Let your customers know you're *alive and kicking* and need their business now.

Too Little Promotion

Promotions can be expensive, inexpensive, or free. In slow times, you'll want to use the second two and spend as little as you can. Similar to free publicity, you want as much exposure as you can get that will generate sales. Promotions can be anything from coupons, contests, scratch cards, exhibits, games, or special events.

One ongoing promotion I've heard about concerns a local pizza restaurant. They offer a 25 percent discount to everyone that cuts out their biggest competitor's ad and brings it in. It must be the original, not copies. This works two ways: the customer gets an immediate discount, and the competitor's ad is no longer in the phone book when the customer is ready to order again. This promotion costs them nothing except a discount that they could have given out with a coupon anyway.

Scratch cards work because they are fun and give the customer or prospect a chance to win something or get a discount. There are stock cards that are low in cost and available quickly. If they bring in more business when you need it most, they're worth the investment. And if scratch cards work well for you, try them again soon or on a regular interval. People will catch on and be waiting for the next time. Prizes or discounts don't have to be large; most people love to win anything. The return rate on scratch cards is much higher than coupons.

If you're a business in a large indoor mall, or in a particular shopping street or district, join in any *joint* sales offers or special events. In a joint effort, the cost of promotion will be shared with all the vendors, and your part will be reasonable. Don't pass up this opportunity to make quick sales and be part of the action.

Promotions of any type will bring attention to your business and remind past customers to visit you again. Most people love to participate in different events rather than the same old 20-percent-off sale. Be creative and find promotions you don't see every day. Be sure to advertise; post signs in your store and send direct mail. You want to create excitement so that potential customers will put you on their to-do list.

CHAPTER 3
Owner Attitude

Remember when your business was doing well? You could sit behind your desk, feet up, hands behind your head, and relax. Relax, because everything was going exactly the way you wanted it to. You were making money and you called the shots. Your customers purchased how and when *you* decided. Competition was scarce—and who would ever think of competing with you? You already had all the business and all the customers. Isn't life great? You set the rules and everyone follows. Maybe you should have shorter business hours so you could have more time off. Customers would have to adjust to your new schedule if they wanted to buy from you. You were the king, and all the peasant customers did your bidding. Now how could you make your job even easier?

Notice anything familiar? Some of the previous examples may seem a little extreme, but similar things happen somewhere every day. If a business owner takes unfair advantage of a situation, then the situation can and will ruin their business in the future. Trying to act better than your customers and looking down on them is a mistake you'll regret. You're forgetting that the customers are really the boss, and you work for them. You're in business to serve their needs, wants, and desires—not yours. An attitude of indifference will make customers feel that you don't care about them and all you want is their money with the least possible effort. No one wants to feel this way when making a purchase. It doesn't matter whether you're the lowest price or the only supplier around, they won't enjoy doing business with you. And if they think this way, they will always be looking for a way out. Whenever the opportunity arises to buy somewhere else (and it will eventually), they are gone. Don't fool yourself; no one *has* to buy from you. There's always an alternative if one looks hard enough.

When you're a new business, you'll do *anything* to get *any* customers. But as a business matures, it starts to take on the personality of its owner. If the owner mentally puts him- or herself on a pedestal, he or she will expect everyone else to do likewise. The attitude of the owner will be conveyed throughout the store, office, email, or on the telephone. Your business personality will reflect your qualities, disposition, and attitude. This can be good or bad depending on the actions of the owner. Customers will pick up on this, and if the attitude and personality is not cordial, friendly, and helpful, it can drive them away. If they don't feel comfortable with the general atmosphere of your business, there's always another place to buy. When this happens too often, your sales will begin to slide and the business is headed for trouble.

You don't want customers thinking or saying it's just too much aggravation to buy from you. And if they begin to feel that way, you can be certain they are telling others. So not only do you have the possibility of losing current customers, but you're also jeopardising prospects who won't even consider your business because of what they've heard. This type of negative word of mouth is the last thing you need. If it sounds like a snowball that keeps getting bigger, that's exactly what it is. Your negative image can grow so fast that it's out of control before you realise it. And if your head is quickly in the clouds, you may not even know that it's happening until it's too late.

Look at some celebrity movie stars and sports figures. They can be revered and celebrated for years, then all of a sudden, a negative story comes out. All the good things in the past are soon forgotten and they are immediately knocked off their pedestal. It may take years to get back on the road to recovery. The same thing can happen to a business and its owner if they are trying to be superior to their customers. Treat your customers the way you did when you first went into business—with the respect and importance they deserve. If you don't, you can be sure that someone else will.

Customer-Friendly Hours

I've seen a lot of stores and businesses suffer sales losses due to inadequate hours of operation. The business is open only when the owner feels it's convenient for him or her, not for the customers. After all, he or she owns the business, why shouldn't he or she set the rules? Well, you're certainly within your rights to do anything you want, but isn't the reason you're in business to make money and grow? You build a prosperous and profitable business by serving the customer, not yourself. If that's not your goal you'd better put up the For Sale sign now while you still can.

If you can't or don't want to keep the hours necessary to accommodate your customers, sell the business and get into a different one. If a customer wants to buy a product at a certain time and you're not open, they will find someone else who is open. They may have been a past customer of yours and never knew about the competition until you forced them to go elsewhere. Now your competitor has their business and there's a good chance that company will get their future business too. And all because you were too stubborn to accommodate them.

Are you willing to take the chance of losing customers just to satisfy yourself? What's the purpose of doing this? The only result will be lost business and lost customers. If you want to leave every day at 5 p.m., but the business needs to be open until 9 p.m., you must find a reliable person or team to handle those extra hours. If customers want to buy during hours you can't or won't be there, you need to find a way to stay open. If there is any technical or product knowledge needed to serve customers there must be a trained person available. Just having the door or phone lines open isn't enough. Remember, great service is not just a check-out queue. This subject is one of my pet peeves, can you tell?

A situation I've seen firsthand that, in my opinion, really helped ruin a business, concerns a children's-wear store. This was the owner's first business, and she decided that she would set the hours that she wanted to work. The problem was that they weren't convenient for the type of customers she needed to attract. She would open at 10 a.m. and close at 6 p.m. everyday and be closed on Sunday. This meant that she was only open when most kids are in school and involved in after-school activities. Should a parent take his or her child out of school or miss gymnastics just to shop at this store? Also, many families have other things planned for Saturday, and mall parking is bad on Saturdays.

We had an ice cream shop two doors down and we drew a lot of families with kids in the evening. We were asked constantly about the children's-wear store and why it wasn't open at least until 8 p.m. And what about all the people who didn't ask, and just left and never returned? One day, when the owner came in our store, I mentioned the fact that people were asking about her shop in the evening. Her response was, "my hours are on the door and if they want to buy at my shop, they have to come when I'm open." She's a nice lady, but had the wrong attitude concerning business hours. Needless to say, the business closed after about a year. It's a shame, because it was a nice-looking shop with beautiful children's clothes. If she only wanted to work eight hours a day, they should have been the hours that customers are available. Many potential purchasers never got a chance to see the unique items she had, except through the window.

Your hours are one of the things you need to consider even before you purchase or open a business. But most new owners ignore the time you need to be available for *all* their customers. Check competitors and remain open for business at least as long as they are, and longer if possible. And if you're not there every day at closing time, make sure your employees aren't shutting down five or 10 minutes early just to help them get out on time. Many times, a customer will rush to be at your place of business right before you close. Don't have the door locked or the voice mail on even a minute before your advertised closing time—and preferably wait five minutes longer.

Make your hours customer-friendly, and it will add to your bottom line. Think of your average sale amount and multiply it out for a year. If you lost one or two sales a day, what would the lost revenue for a year be? Work it out; you may be surprised at how big the numbers are. And those lost customers won't be sending any of their friends, either.

Your Attitude Will Transfer to Employees

As I said before, the business will begin to take on the personality of its owner. This can be good or bad, and customers will recognise it. They will see it in your employees because they will begin to act and treat customers the way you do. The old "do as I say, not as I do" doesn't work anymore in today's marketplace. Employees look to you, the owner, as the example they should follow. They will pick up your bad habits as well as some of your good ones. If you act indifferent or superior to customers and prospects, they will assume it's okay for them to act that way also.

Little by little, your entire company will assume that what the owner does is the way it should be. Once employees get an unfriendly attitude, it will be hard to change them. If the owner wakes up one day and realises that there's a problem with attitude in the business, it may be too late to reverse it. Some employees will be set in their ways because it was accepted in the past. The situation may be serious enough to require the owner to replace some of them. Of course, the best solution is not to let it happen in the first place. So if your employees all seem to have an attitude problem, look in the mirror and see if that's where it's coming from.

Shut-Down? What's That?

Many industrial and manufacturing companies feel they need to shut down all operations and abandon all customers for a week or more every year. Why? Just because it's convenient to have everyone take their holidays at the same time? They try to pick a slow time of the year to do it. But is there really a slow time when a customer has a rush order or special situation? What should they do, change their entire business to accommodate yours? Not everyone can or will plan ahead so that they won't need your company during the time you specify. Why should they anyway? It's not up to you to decide how your customers run *their* business. And what about that new prospect you've been trying to sell to for the last six months? What if they are ready to order and take a chance on your company, but need to order during your shut-down?

The probable answer to all these questions is that they will go to your competitors, who have been waiting for this to happen, and if they are smart, they won't have a shut-down to reciprocate. Customers who are forced to try competitors that they never purchased from before will be a little uneasy at first. If they have become comfortable as your customer, they may feel betrayed because you have abandoned them temporarily. But if they must buy while you're closed, they will get to see how others in your industry will serve them. They will experience doing business with someone that they may have only heard about. But what if they find that the fear of the unknown isn't so bad after all?

They are getting the same quality product or service at a comparative price, or—oh no—a lower price! Well, you know what happens next: they stay with their new source, and your company is soon forgotten. Chalk up another lost customer to the owner's attitude. Why allow something like this to happen?

Why not find a better way. There always is one if you look hard enough. What about sending only a quarter of your staff on holiday at a time? Then you will have three-quarters left to process orders and accommodate customers. Pick your slowest time of the year and let everyone in your business know well in advance. If you have the time to schedule everyone for the week they choose, your employees will be more receptive to this arrangement. I'm a firm believer that closing a business down at *any* time of the year is a mistake that will hurt you in the long run. Customers need to purchase at all different times, and you need to be able to accommodate them.

Too Busy for Your Customers

A lot of people will use a small shop or order from a small business because they can meet the owner once in a while. They know if they have a serious problem with a purchase, they can get to the person who can and will resolve it. But if the owner is not available or too busy, it creates a bad impression that sometimes is not forgotten. Most of the time, customers want to say hello and be acknowledged for their patronage. After all, they know who ultimately receives the profits for their business. Even on the phone, when the customer is many miles away, it's nice to become part of the ordering process and talk to the people who make your business possible. This will help reinforce a bond between your company and its customers, especially when sales are slow. You want everyone who buys from you to know that you appreciate their purchase and want them to be completely satisfied. And who better to convey this message than the person at the top. A "thank you for your business" goes a long way.

But what if the owner doesn't participate and won't talk to customers? Can this really affect sales and repeat orders? Sure it can, because in a smaller business, customers know you can be available if you want to. You may be busy, but not so busy that you can't spend even 20 to 30 seconds with someone. If your company is a major multinational, customers know they can't reach the top people. Actually, most of the top people in large corporations don't even know who their customers are, and don't really care to find out. They look more at numbers that affect their stock price and forget where those numbers come from. Your smaller company is different and your customers know it. They know you can find some time to talk to them if you really want to. If you're hiding in a back office or behind a phone, the impression comes across that you really don't care. This may not seem like a big issue to some owners, but if you lose even a few customers because of it, why let that happen? Think of what it has cost to get even one new customer.

I used to visit a fine-dining restaurant that was close to my home and had great food and atmosphere; I got to know the owner. We went there about twice a month and usually spent around £60 on dinner for two, including drinks. The owner would see us and stop at our table for a little small talk and see if everything was okay. He asked how the food was and if we had any requests for fresh fish or other main courses in the future. The one to two minutes he spent was enough, and made me feel important. After I moved out of the area, I still thought of the restaurant and vowed to go back when I had the chance. It took three years for me to get back there, but I found time to visit the restaurant on a Saturday night.

A few of the people there remembered me, and I thought the same owner would be happy to see me. I was sure he knew me by name because I was a loyal patron for so many years. I asked our waiter to let him know I was here, and hoped he would stop at the table for a couple of minutes. But to my dismay, the waiter advised me that though he remembered me too, he was too busy in the office and could not come down. He knew we'd travelled a great distance and made a special effort to find the time to return to his restaurant. Maybe there was another reason that stopped him from coming over. I don't really know, but I felt put off that he couldn't find even 30 seconds to acknowledge my presence. I just don't feel the same about wanting to go back when I'm in town. The food was still very good, but the important feeling of being there was gone. I don't think I'll make an effort to go back again.

However, I went back to another restaurant the next day that I often ate at during lunch. It's one of my favourite Chinese restaurants, family owned and not too big. When I walked in after three years, they recognised me right away (even with the extra 10lbs), and the first question was, "Where have you been? We missed you!" They gave me one of my favourite tables and within three minutes, the owner came over and sat across from me for almost five minutes, asking how I was and what I was doing. The bill for food here is a lot less than the expensive restaurant, but the way I was treated, they will make it in the long run. Whenever I'm in town, which is now about three to four times a year, I'll find time to stop there for a pleasant Chinese lunch or dinner. They make me feel important and find time to talk to me even when it's busy. I always recommend them to anyone who asks about a Chinese restaurant.

The second example is the way you build customer loyalty and get repeat business and referrals. The owner realises it takes a little more than great products and services to make a business survive and prosper during good and bad times. Make customers feel that recognition for their continued patronage comes directly from the top. Don't be too busy or uninterested in talking to the people who keep you in business.

You Don't Want to Go Home Late

Everyone is tired and ready to leave when a long day is over. But there are correct and foolish ways to close your business for the day. Don't be so strict with your hours that you shut out a possible customer just because it's closing time. You don't really know how much effort a person has gone through to try to make it before you close. It's normal for the Post Office to close their door, exactly at the time listed, but not your small business. Why turn away business at the last minute just because the clock is now at your stated closing time? They didn't come all the way over to your business to be turned away. The small business owner needs to realise that these people who are trying to purchase from you are valuable assets you can't afford to lose. The few extra minutes it takes to serve them is insignificant compared to the lifetime value of a satisfied customer.

Here's a horror story about closing before your scheduled time. As I've mentioned, we once owned an ice cream shop, and about a quarter of a mile away was one of the new-style stores that *mixes in* the toppings. It seems popular, especially in warm weather. They serve much more slowly than our scoop store, so it always looks busy there. We may serve the same number of customers, because we could handle about two in the time it takes them to serve one. Both shops closed at the same time. Only the other shop stops taking orders about 10 minutes before closing so they can finish right on time. Many people get shut out, so they would come to our store because we would stay open until everyone was served. One night, a family of four came and told us that the other shop served the father and two children, but when it was the wife's turn, they said "sorry, no more". Of course we served her and they came back to our shop several times. We've heard similar stories to this one, in which they would serve part of a group, but not all of them because of closing time. They were allowing us to build our business as a result of their mistakes. Their business is still good, but if they continue with this attitude, it will suffer in the long run.

Walk-Ins

And what about walk-ins if your business is mostly done by reservations or appointments? These last-minute patrons could be some of your best future customers if you can find a way to accommodate them now. They may have just accidentally found your business, but need what you sell right away. Why punish them for not following your regular procedure? Find a way to serve their need and build a long-term loyal customer.

These are all owner attitude problems and can affect the health and prosperity of the entire business. What if this happens to some of your best regular customers? How long will they stay around and put up with situations they don't like? Competitors are always waiting to offer that extra effort if you won't. They want your customers and don't really care if your business falls into troubled times. Don't make it too easy for them.

CHAPTER 4

Poor Employee Training and Supervision

Today's companies are much leaner than ever before when it comes to the number of employees; small companies are no exception to this new rule of reduced personnel. Company owners want the same work done by fewer employees, but are they sacrificing quality and customer care in the process? Not necessarily, if the proper training and supervision is part of the game plan. Employees can be only as good as you train them to be. And they will only stay good with proper encouragement and supervision. When employee performance slides, it can take company growth and repeat sales with it. In many cases, it's only human nature for your employees to do the least acceptable job that you will tolerate. By tolerating below-par job performance from even a few employees, it will infect your entire company. If it's too much trouble for you, the owner, to care, why should they?

Initial training and the consistent reinforcement of that training is the key to top employee performance. If you don't enforce employees' training and supervise their actions, it will be easily forgotten. When supervision is lacking, people will begin to do things the way *they* want to, not how they were trained. Observing employees, in the process of doing their job, will quickly tell you whether a refresher class is necessary. You will know right away if they are performing their jobs the way you intended it to be done. But if you do nothing to correct the situation, don't be surprised if it starts to hurt your business. If you think it's too much trouble to change now, wait until you try to reverse a sales decline. Your employees are probably streetwise, so why shouldn't you be also?

Employees, similar to everyone else, get set in their ways. The longer you let poor job performance go on, the harder it will be to correct later. It's a shame if you have to terminate the contract of an employee who won't change now because you let things go unchecked.

The following are some excuses why employees don't follow your job guidelines and policies, and what to do about it:

- They think it's not important—this results from not stressing how their performance adds to the overall health of the business.
- They want to do things their way—you need to emphasise the need to join the proven team effort. When everyone works together and does their job the way they were trained, it makes the company stronger.
- They don't know what to do—this can result from two things. Either their initial training was not adequate and tested, or they didn't pay attention or care to learn. If it's the second reason, you need to watch these employees carefully.
- It's too much effort—this is a quality of lazy people who will only do the minimum to get by, or less than the minimum if no one supervises them. Try to weed out these people at the interview stage and don't put them in customer service.
- They forget how to do things—they either don't care to remember, or haven't done their task long enough to make it habit forming. Some people learn faster than others, and you need to bear with the slower ones if you see that they really care about their job.
- They don't believe in your methods—if you have a proven system, you need to make employees understand and believe in it. The person who just doesn't care needs to look elsewhere for work. You just can't afford to have someone who is bucking the system.
- No one will find out—this is the attitude of sneaky people who will take advantage of any situation they can. If they have little or no supervision, there's no telling what

they may or may not do. Keep an eye on them and motivate them.

- Poor performance is not reprimanded—if you know that certain employees are not doing their job the way you want it done, you must correct them. By letting things just go on, it says that you approve and everything is okay.

- You have the wrong person for the job—if you become aware of this and see potential in the employee, transfer him or her to a position that better fits his or her abilities. You don't want to put a shy or quiet person in customer service.

- The job is monotonous or boring—no one wants to put a square peg in a square hole for eight hours a day. Try to offer some variety in each job, or train employees in several jobs and move them around occasionally. They should perform better.

- Why they do certain things—do they need to know the purpose of their job and how it fits into the big picture? You can offer a brief reason why what they are doing is important and why you need them to do it well.

- No reward for doing a good job—of course, keeping their job and getting paid is what they expect. But other little perks and recognition can make an employee feel special, and encourage them to keep up the good work.

- Company morale is low—this problem starts at the top with the owners themselves. If the owner is negative and always down in the dumps, the employees will feel the same. Even a company experiencing tough times can maintain a positive attitude with its employees.

- Employees have no input—"keep quiet and do your job" is not going to build a healthy staff. Give employees a chance to offer ideas about their job and how to do it better. This can be done at meetings, or face-to-face with their immediate supervisor.

Open-Door Policy

As the owner of a small business, you have the responsibility of listening to all your employees. This doesn't mean that if you have 30 people that they all can bring their problems to you every day. But it does mean that if there are difficult matters and unanswered questions that can't be resolved by other supervisory personnel, you *need* to be available. You have to remember that what may seem trivial to you may be of great importance to an employee. People have different needs, and those needs should be resolved on their level.

Unhappy, neglected, or ignored employees are not going to put the 100 percent effort into their job that you need in order to get out of a business slump. If people are doing the minimum, it will show in quality and service. Many times, it only takes a few minutes of listening to a problem or situation to get them back on the right track.

If you're very busy or away from your shop or office a lot, you still need to find time to listen to your employees. You can try to schedule an hour or so twice a week when you're available and put aside everything else. This will show your people you really care and want to help any way you can. Having a short meeting to handle any employee problems or enquiries is just as important as any other business meeting. Employees need to know they are not just a number on a payroll list.

You can set up a procedure for employees to follow when they have questions, problems, or grievances. But your door should be open to get involved with any situations that can't be resolved elsewhere. Your help and decisions need to be fair, honest, and in the best interests of the company *and* the employee. Needless to say, anything personal or confidential should be kept private or in locked personnel files. You want your employees to feel good when they leave your office, and return to their job with enthusiasm. You may have other business problems, but listening to your employees should be on your priority list. It's your employees, more than you realise, that can help you get through tough times.

How Much Training Is the Right Amount?

I'm sure you've walked into a shop or called a company on the phone and the person you end up with doesn't know the answers to your questions. They might only know the common answers for the common products. They can't help you make a decision or suggest what is best for your situation. If a more experienced back-up person is not with them, you have to wait until they're available. This wastes your valuable time and makes you wonder if you're buying from the right company. Why is a person who is not fully trained or fully knowledgeable trying to help a new customer? You really have no idea at first who your new customer is, so they must be given all the expertise your business has to offer.

So how much training is really necessary? How long should it take and who should do it? Training should last:

- As long as it takes to learn how to work with a customer professionally.

- Long enough for an employee to answer most of the questions a customer might bring up, and feel comfortable doing it.

- Long enough to know all about the company's products and services.

- Long enough to know the products' benefits and advantages, and which ones are best suited to a customer's needs.

The customer looks to your people as experts in your industry, and wants to rely on their advice. If the people they are working with are unsure of themselves or their answers, it reflects on the entire business. It's like telling the customer, "try us at your own risk". How many of us really want that? Think of how one under-prepared employee makes the rest of the staff look. Does anyone except the owner really know what's going on here?

These situations, although much too common, are what can hold a business back from growing. When difficult times come or spending is tight, customers want to receive the most for their money. People will still make purchases, but will be more selective of where and with whom. If your company and its employees don't measure up, you can expect lost sales. And too many lost sales will soon bring other problems.

They Don't Get Any Respect!

If you have trained your employees correctly and reinforce that training with tune-up meetings, you can sit back and relax, right? Wrong, because if you don't go one step further, you'll be doing it all over again due to turnover. Many small businesses have great employees who do an admirable job and really care about the company. So, what do you give them in return? A wage, the right to keep their job, and an occasional holiday? Streetwise employers know people want more, even if it's little things that aren't financial.

If you want your employees to give that extra effort that makes great companies, you need to show them you appreciate it. Employees need to be treated with dignity, trust, and respect. And if you give them these things, you'll see that they will, as a result, earn it. At some time in your past, you worked for a company you didn't own. How were you treated? Did your job performance relate to that treatment? Did your supervisor or boss praise good work or only reprimand poor work? And how did you feel when they said "good job" or "well done"? The people who work for you know and feel the same. If they make an effort to do a little more than is expected, they want to know that you noticed.

The attitude and actions of your employees can make or break a business that's going through tough times. You want them all on your side, not against you. The company will have a much better chance of recovery if employees work together as a team for the overall good of the company. To get them to do that, you need to let them know that you really need their full support. When the company is back on its feet and prospering, everyone who participated will share the rewards. And when they help you turn the company around, don't forget to have a "mission accomplished" party.

No Tolerance Policy

Employees are human beings too, and have good days and bad days like you do. The best people on your staff know how to control the bad days and other temptations that everyone gets. It's the ones that can't exercise personal restraint that must be dealt with quickly and severely with a zero tolerance policy. Zero tolerance means that something will get done with no questions asked. The policy you establish can be immediate dismissal, suspension without pay, or sending them home on-the-spot for the rest of the day. Whatever your policy, it should be known by all your employees, so there is no doubt as to what will happen, and no exceptions.

Some instances of unacceptable behaviour can be more serious than others. You need to decide what sort of discipline is correct for each one. But if more than one person is guilty of the same offence, they must be treated the same. It doesn't matter whether they are in management or on the shop floor; job performance has nothing to do with it. Some of the things you will need a zero tolerance policy for are:

- Stealing from the company.
- Deliberate accounting errors.
- Sexual harassment.
- Poor treatment of customers.
- Drug or alcohol abuse.
- Swearing and inappropriate jokes.
- Destroying office equipment.
- Unacceptable personal hygiene.
- Accepting bribes from customers or suppliers.
- Insubordination.
- Lying or cheating about time worked.

I'm sure you can add a few more to the list that directly apply to your business. The important thing is that you act swiftly and harshly when one of these occurs. The rest of your staff will know that serious incidents will not be taken lightly. It's a shame that it takes an example to get the point across, but if that's what it takes, do it.

Have a Suggestion Box for Employees

As old fashioned as it sounds, having a suggestion box still works because it gives employees an outlet to voice their opinions. And by having a specific place or box for them to submit, it shows you are really interested in what they have to say. Your employees see your business from a different perspective than you do, especially the job they do every day. Their ideas and suggestions about your business are better than you'll get from any expensive consulting firm. Most people will give you their observations and opinions based on current and past experiences. They will want to make their job easier or more rewarding as well as benefit the company overall.

The ideas and suggestions should be read and reviewed at least weekly. Don't wait a month—that's way too long and those suggestions could have already been put to good use. I think that these suggestions should be read first in private by the owner and supervisory staff. This will eliminate a poor or silly one from being publicly broadcast in front of other employees. You don't want to embarrass anyone in front of

55

his or her co-workers. Once you feel the suggestion has some merit, you can then toss it out for discussion at an employee meeting.

When you get one of those great "why didn't I think of that" ideas from an employee, you need to do three things right away:

- Acknowledge and thank the employee publicly.
- Give some type of reward or compensation.
- Put the idea into practice ASAP.

Don't sit around with a great idea or suggestion for months the way big companies do. Use it as soon as you can or start testing to see what the best way to implement it is. If your business is currently having difficulties, a good kick start from a new idea may be what it takes to get you on the road to recovery. Your next hope will be that other employees will observe all the excitement this created and start submitting more great ideas of their own.

Don't underestimate the power and value of loyal employees. Many of them can help you more than by just *doing a job*. But unless you show them that you're really interested in what they have to say, why should they bother?

CHAPTER 5
Paying Suppliers Slowly

Paying your suppliers should be in the top three of your payment priority list, right behind employees and taxes, and before rent in most cases. You can always find another shop or office from which to run your business, but it's hard to find a new supplier that you're comfortable with. Keeping good suppliers of merchandise and services is important because of their consistency and value to you *and* your customers. When cash flow gets tight and your payment cycle gets longer, you can end up with orders on hold. Without products shipping to you or your customers, business comes to a standstill. When you change suppliers for any reason, there is always a break-in period for both sides to adjust. In most cases, a new supplier will ask you for a deposit or prepayment on the first order or a couple of orders.

Your suppliers are your lifeline to what you sell to your customers. You may not be able to do business without them. They supply you with the products, parts, and services you need to resell, manufacture, or service your customers.

No Suppliers=No Products=No Customers

What comes in the back door goes out the front door, and you make a profit in between. Sounds so simple, doesn't it? But if there's a break or stoppage of this flow, then the entire operation comes to a halt. Even professional companies such as doctor's offices, law offices, and accounting firms need products and services from outsiders to be able to perform their jobs effectively. Doctors need medical supplies and lab services, and professional services need office supplies, payroll, and tax processing.

You can take the viewpoint that you're the supplier's customer, so you call the shots. But once a comfortable relationship has been established, it's difficult and time consuming to change. So when tough times happen and you don't have money to pay everyone all that's due, what can you do? Hopefully, this chapter will give you some ideas that may work in your cash shortage situation. Mark the ideas that can work for you so you can refer back to them in the future if the need arises again.

Getting Behind on the Bills

This happens to all of us at one time or another, and it's probably unavoidable. For your business though, it can be a little more serious, and you need to watch it more closely. If you ignore the fact that you're getting behind on supplier bills, it will only get worse and maybe even out of control. Keep a physical and/or computer file of all bills received, and date them. Use a rubber stamp or automatic date stamp and record the day you receive them. Invoices can come in the mail, via fax, or by email. Once your incoming invoices are dated and approved, you need some type of system to keep track of the oldest ones and when they are due. Most small business computer accounting programs will do this for you. The bills should be entered into the computer program as soon as possible after you receive them. If you're still using a manual system, have different files for suppliers and expenses. And if you have a major supplier with a lot of invoices for your purchases, make a separate file for them.

Review all your supplier bills often, at least once a week, to see what's still open and due. This will also make you aware of any large invoices coming. A large supplier invoice should be a priority when it comes to deciding who gets paid and when. If cash flow is tight, a larger invoice must still be paid in order to keep working with this supplier. Take a look at your daily cash receipts and figure out a way to get this one off the books. The further in advance you know about it, the better chance you'll have to take care of it. Don't hide your head in the sand and ignore suppliers' invoices. Know what you owe even if you can't pay them everything on time, and let your suppliers' accounting department know that you may be a little late.

At one company I had in the past, the salesperson would need to approve a supplier's invoice and transfer the information to our billing department. We would then invoice our customer as soon as possible. Then the approved supplier invoice would be turned over to our computer and accounting person, who would enter it into our accounts payable. Out of the five sales people we had, one was very lax about turning in the approved suppliers' invoices. Occasionally, he or she would either leave them on his or her messy desk, put them in a drawer, or accidentally toss them out with other waste paper. After about 45 days, we'd get a call inquiring why a specific invoice wasn't paid. When we couldn't find a record of it anywhere, we questioned the salesperson, whose response was "I don't know." After some investigating, we found unentered bills in a drawer totalling more than £10,000. This was money we owed and weren't aware of on our accounts payable reports. The salesperson was reprimanded and eventually left the company. We found a few smaller cases with other salespeople and made sure that *everyone* knew the correct procedure. We instilled a new rule that the supplier invoice had to be attached to our customer billing form when it was turned in for invoicing. That way it was out of the salesperson's hands right away.

This example shows how you can be deceived into believing you have more money than you really do. When hidden or unentered bills surface unexpectedly, they can put a lot of stress on your cash flow. And they always seem to show up when they're already overdue, which gives you less time to deal with them. You need to put some safeguards into place so this doesn't happen to you. It's hard enough when sales and cash flow are down; you don't need anything unforeseen to creep up on you. It makes it more difficult to deal with a troublesome situation when you can't see the entire picture. You need all the information you can get, whether good or bad, to make intelligent and useful decisions. When you trust someone to provide this information, don't just assume that it's being done exactly as you specify. As time goes by, they might find shortcuts and "I'll do it tomorrow's" that countermand the procedures you originally set up. You need to periodically check to see that all invoices are being processed the way you designate. Don't take anything for granted and end up in a more serious situation.

Know Your Supplier's Real Terms

Let's say you have 20 regular suppliers and another 10 or 15 that you use from time to time. The casual supplier, although important, won't put you out of business if it stops doing business with you. And there are probably alternative sources where you can order the same products or services. But your 20 regular suppliers are the lifeblood of your company, and losing one of them could hamper your business. You've come to rely on them and you need what they sell you to properly service your customers. But each of them will have different, unwritten terms of payment, and you need to know what they are.

Your first intention should be to pay all your suppliers on time and within terms. But let's face it, business has its ups and downs, and paying everyone on time is not always possible. If every small business person always had enough money to pay all bills on time, then this book wouldn't be necessary. Life is not that kind to all of us, so we need to work on the issues that are sometimes swept under the carpet.

You need to know which of your regular suppliers are going to put the most pressure on, and which will be more lax and understanding. You can find this out by doing business with them throughout a period of time. You'll probably have minor slow times and be a few days late paying an invoice. Some suppliers will be on the phone to you or your accounting person the day after the terms end and expect immediate payment. Others will wait several more days or send a reminder via mail, fax, or email. Others send a monthly statement showing details of your invoices at the bottom, then follow up a few days later with a phone call. Still others will do nothing and let you pay when you can. There aren't too many of these nice guys that let you pay when you can, but they are out there. Just don't take unfair advantage of them; pay quickly when you can. If you don't pay them at all or don't send them something periodically, they will quickly change and start demanding quick payment or hold orders for payment of old invoices. You want to avoid a supplier from *holding* your orders at all costs. This action can prevent you from servicing your customer and getting repeat business. And when times are slow, you can't afford to lose any business, especially from repeat customers.

So break your suppliers into four groups, either mentally or on paper. Don't keep this list on your computer where anyone in your office can get access to it. This is priority information that is for the owner's eyes only. Employees and accounting people will have an idea of which suppliers put on the most pressure, but it won't be written down anywhere. Your personal list can be:

- Pay within terms.
- Quick, nonverbal reminders.
- Statements with call follow-up.
- "Nice guys" who will wait.

You can then make a second list and rank all your regular suppliers in order of importance to your business. There will be some that you just can't stay in business without, who will head the list and so on, all the way down to the least essential ones at the bottom. Then compare this list with your real payment terms list and see where the top of the list falls. You can only hope that your most essential suppliers don't fall into your "pay within terms" category. But if they do, you have to deal with it and keep your orders moving.

When cash flow is tight, you can call your top suppliers and talk to your highest contact (preferably not in accounting) and see if he or she will give you a little breathing room. Even five or 10 days longer can do a lot of good in allocating the funds you have available. Sometimes the past orders, if regular and of good size, will get your contact to budge a little and help you for a short period of time. Any loyalty you've built up throughout the years can pay off now when you need it most. Don't be afraid to ask, even if it's an unpleasant call to make. Its part of owning your own business and necessary to the health of your company. And the owner or top-level management person should make the call, not a lower-level employee.

Keep Orders Moving

If you want to stay in business and recover from any slump you're experiencing, you need to keep suppliers' orders moving. Whether it's incoming stock to your shop, parts you need for assembly, or orders shipping directly to your customers, keep them moving. Any break in the cycle will hold you back even further and interrupt your collection and billing of customers. Plus, your customers will experience late deliveries and unstocked shelves, which are terrible for customer care and repeat orders. You don't want this to happen, and must have a plan to head it off before it does. You should be aware of what your suppliers will do if you get behind on their invoices. Some will hold current and future orders, and some will not. The logic is that you will have to pay old invoices to keep orders shipping. And of course, they're right, you need your orders to make new profits and keep your business in business.

If you know that an important supplier has the policy of holding orders when even one invoice passes a certain number of days old, you must pay it before that time. If you just can't pay it, call your supplier and let your contact know when you will pay. An extension of only five or 10 days may allow the supplier to release your order(s) after the usual *hold* time. But if you say nothing and hope no one notices, you're fooling yourself. With today's computer accounting programs, suppliers won't miss it by more than a day or so. Your best chance is to call a few days before the *hold* deadline and plead your case. If you're a several-year customer who has paid fairly well in the past, your chances of working something out are reasonably good. Just don't wait until the last day to call, or worse yet, make the supplier call you.

If an order gets held up because of past payment, you create several problems, such as:

1. An unhappy customer who isn't going to get their order in the time you originally specified. You'll have to come up with some excuse because you won't want to tell them the real reason.

2. A loss of a current order or cash sale because you can't honestly bill someone for an order that's not shipped. You'll have to wait longer to collect the profit on this sale.

3. A chance of empty shelves in your shop, or customer back orders for popular products. Customers hate to wait and may go elsewhere to purchase if you don't have it in stock or get it quickly.

4. An unhappy supplier because they are waiting for you to pay past invoices, which affects *their* cash flow. It's also extra work to hold an order and make sure it's not released until authorised.

5. An unhappy supplier *again* because they have a finished product or in-process order that they can't ship. They

have to find a place to store it until released. Additional time is wasted.

6. An unhappy owner because you need the profit and cash flow from any orders on hold to pay bills and suppliers. It also takes up valuable mental time and paperwork to keep track of.

Does it sound like everyone's angry with you? Well, maybe they are, even if you're trying hard to rectify the situation. Orders on hold can be a time-consuming and frustrating situation that you want to avoid whenever possible. Many times, a little advance planning and proper allocation of your available money can help prevent these conditions from happening. And once an order is held, you become sort of a marked customer with the suppliers, and they will watch your payment activity a lot closer in the near future. It will probably take six months to a year to get back in their comfort zone again. And if they belong to a close association or industry credit interchange, your other suppliers may soon find out what has taken place. If you're working in a small niche industry, everyone knows each other and credit risks circulate quickly. If you resolve the *order on hold* situation right away, you can probably avoid being put on the watch list. If you don't pay one supplier, others in the same industry will find out about it if there's a secure website available to members of their credit interchange. You may have difficulty ordering from anyone in the industry without prepayment.

Take the Calls

When you get behind with suppliers that are important, but not the highest on your must-use list, they will be calling and inquiring about payment. These calls should first go to the person who handles your accounting, or to your assistant. If you don't have such a person, then it's you. You could designate one person to take these calls and explain that things are slow and you will try to pay their invoice as soon as you can. This should hold them off for at least a week before they call again. When they call back, your designated person can attempt the same excuse and try to offer a projected time when you can send payment. If you just can't pay by the time you hoped to and they call again (you know they will), try to offer a partial payment to show you're really trying to pay, but just can't send the full amount. More than likely they will accept the partial payment, and this should buy you another week to 10 days. This can be repeated over and over until it's finally fully paid. Be sure that the person you designate *takes* the calls, and if using voice mail, returns calls the same day. The one thing that really alarms a supplier trying to collect an invoice is the inability to reach someone.

What if the supplier calls you, the owner, directly? Will you be too busy to take the call? No, you take the call or return it promptly if you're not in. You want to save this relationship if you can, not destroy it. You may not have anything new to tell them, but hearing it from the top person can make a difference. Assure them that you want to pay in full and you will if given more time. Offer to set up a payment plan that you know you can handle. The more often you send partial payments, the less they should call. I think frequent smaller payments are better than trying to pay big chunks at a time. If you owe £1,000, see if you can send only £100 a week until it's paid off. They will look at every payment they receive as money they didn't lose if something major goes wrong in your company.

The one thing you don't want to do is lie to your suppliers. It's better to tell the truth about any problems you're having, but with an optimistic outlook. Everyone likes to hear that everything will be okay eventually. The problem with lying is that you'll probably have to tell more lies to cover up the previous ones. And what if you can't remember what lie you told to whom? With the truth, there's only one answer, and it's easy to remember what you said.

Asking for your suppliers' help is another way of throwing the ball back into their court. Let them know that you want to pay and continue your business relationship, but need some help with how to do it. Briefly explain your current situation and that cash flow is slower than normal. There's not much available to pay all the bills you want to. But don't make their invoice sound any less important than other bigger suppliers you have. You want them to feel that they are just as significant as everyone else. Ask them how you can work this out and still keep doing business together. You may be surprised at their response, because they should want to help in any way they can. It's in their best interests to collect this debt and keep you as a future customer. It's the company that won't take their collection calls and send partial payments that they want to get rid of. I remember a teacher in the past telling me that "it never hurts to ask". The worst answer you can get is no, and that's unlikely. Remember, suppliers don't want to put you out of business; they just want to be paid. There may be some concessions they're willing to offer that you didn't think of. So ask for their help and use it to keep your business on the right track.

Use Order Deposits

When you're selling business to business and you acquire a new customer, asking for a deposit on the first order is not an unusual practice. Most business customers will agree to this, and credit cards make it even easier. In several of my businesses, we ask for a 50 percent deposit and the balance after the order is shipped. That 50 percent deposit includes some of your profit, so there's really more than half of your cost. You can send about 80 percent of what you receive to your supplier, who will either make the product or ship parts to you for your manufacturing. The balance of what you receive can be used to pay other invoices or expenses. When the supplier invoice becomes due, you will then owe only the balance after the deposit you sent. The money in advance will make the supplier feel comfortable and help smooth out any past situations.

Deposits can also be requested of retail customers when they are purchasing special order merchandise or larger than normal orders that are not cash-and-carry. Most people will understand that a deposit is necessary, and it shouldn't be a problem. This advance money, or most of it, can also be forwarded to your supplier as a deposit or used to pay old bills with them. When the order is complete, retail customers usually pay the balance without any extended terms, so you should be able to pay the supplier in full for this order.

Planning From Experience

If you feel as though you're backed into a corner with no way out—and I mean really feel your company is in trouble—you'll have to try more drastic methods. If you want to save your business, and you've tried everything you could think of, here's another idea that I have used in the past. This is not an idea to be taken lightly, and should only be used as a last resort when you've already been unsuccessful at other methods. This idea is not for everyone and every situation, but if it can help, here it is.

First, you must feel that your company would have a good chance of recovery if all those supplier bills were off your back, at least for a while. If you don't think your company will make it, even if the supplier overdues are out of the picture, then this method probably won't work. In that case, you should consider reorganization or closing the business (Chapter 24). But if you can see the light at the end of the tunnel and don't want to give up, then keep trying. Many a company in trouble was saved by a persistent or resolute owner. If you're not afraid to try something new, you have a chance. But if you can't stand the heat, get out of the…well, you know.

When you get to a point at which you know you can't possibly pay your old supplier bills with current cash flow and current business, you have to do something. Taking collection calls (don't avoid them) is taking up a lot of your time. Time that could be used to go after more business and new customers. When you're slow paying your bills for a while, suppliers will know you're having problems and hope you can come up with a plan. Remember that they just want to be paid and continue doing business with you. And you want to pay them when you can and continue doing business also. But right now, you've reached a point you know is leading to a dead end unless you act soon. I've been at this point and tried a plan that I didn't know whether it would work or destroy our company.

I sat in my office and wrote a professional standard letter to my suppliers. I wanted it to look like a standard letter so each supplier was being contacted and treated like everyone else. In the letter, I explained that we were having financial problems and our bank credit line was at its limit. I also wanted to sound optimistic, so I said that business was picking up, and with a little help now, the future looked very promising. I made a list of non-fixed expenses and showed how we planned to reduce them as much as possible, giving a percentage for each one. I also said I was going to reduce my own salary by 40 percent and eliminate some of the perks I was getting. I wanted to state all the things we were willing to do before I requested what I needed from them. This letter might alarm a few suppliers, but most of them knew the current situation.

To help us get back on our feet and save the company, we needed some concessions from all the suppliers receiving this letter. Without most of them on our side, the plan wouldn't work. So in the next section of the letter, I listed what we needed to help us recover:

1. All invoices that are more than 30 days old would be put aside for 90 to 120 days with no payment due until then.

2. We would pay invoices less than 30 days old on time using the current cash flow that we had.

3. Suppliers would keep shipping orders to us and our customers as long as we kept the current invoices current.

4. We would still receive our priority pricing and discounts so we could remain competitive in the marketplace.

5. We would start paying off the older invoices that were put aside after 90 to 120 days. We would pay 5 or 10 percent of the amount owed per month until everything was paid.

When you get to number five, be realistic. Don't promise more than you can handle or you'll end up right back where you started. You know your suppliers better than anyone, and should have a feeling of how far you can push it.

What you're really offering them is a way you can pay them everything you owe them and still continue giving them new business. Before this letter, they were only getting excuses or reasons why you *couldn't pay*. Now, you're making an offer of a plan of how you *can pay*. Believe me, they don't want to see you go out of business any more than you do. If your company closes, they know that they will get next to nothing, plus lose any future business from you. If they accept your plan, there's a good chance they will get the entire amount within a reasonable time.

At the end of the letter, leave a place where they can write their company name, date, and sign to show acceptance. Give a deadline when they need to respond, and ask them to fax it back to you as soon as possible. Request an answer even if it's a no, so you know where you stand with each one. If some don't respond, you should call them and explain what you are trying to do.

Once you write and send this letter, there's no turning back, and you can't change your mind. You've laid it all out on the table for everyone to see, so don't be bashful now. Some suppliers or their credit department personnel may call you to discuss the letter. Be prepared and available to honestly answer all their questions. If possible, invite them to your shop or office to see firsthand what you're trying to do. Remember, you're asking them to agree to something they don't do every day. A decision to agree to what you proposed is not going to be made by their credit department. Someone higher up in the organization needs to make this decision. You can also offer to visit them at their company if it's in your local area. Don't spend valuable money flying around the country; handle those suppliers by phone. Let them know you need the collection calls to stop so you can get back to marketing and selling to increase your cash flow.

There will be a few suppliers who won't agree to your plan, but you have to deal with them. If they respond with a no, make a personal attempt to contact the highest-level person you know there and plead your case. If you don't know any of the top people, ask to speak to the president or owner. When this person finds out what you're calling about, he or she should be willing to talk to you. Let him or her know that without his or her help, the plan will be less effective.

There will still be suppliers who just won't budge and won't ship your orders until you pay your old invoices. At this point, you have to look elsewhere for a supplier from which you can get a similar product or service at a comparable price. Or can you operate your business without replacing them at all? Can you discontinue selling what you used them for, especially if it was a low-profit item? This is the time to make any changes necessary to improve the health of your business. You can't let one or two stubborn suppliers jeopardise your recovery efforts. And if you just do nothing, you'll never have a chance to get back to a normal business atmosphere.

When bills and suppliers start closing in, you have to do something. Whether it's this plan or one of your own, take some action before things get even worse. Have a short meeting with your top three or four suppliers and brainstorm together. As I said previously, it's in their best interests to help you. And for the very few who refuse to help, shut them out of future business. Because once your company has solved all its problems, everyone will want you as their customer. This is the time to show your loyalty to all the suppliers who were there when you needed them. Don't abandon them for a small price difference when they helped you through your worst times.

CHAPTER 6
Excessive Spending

Wouldn't you like to close your company for a week and take all your employees and their significant others on a Caribbean cruise? You only live once, and you need to live for the moment. Your customers will have to wait because you need a break from the normal routine, and the company owes it to you. There's money in the bank, so why not use it? When you get back, customers will be lined up begging you to take their orders or to make purchases. Why didn't you think of this before? You could be doing this every year!

It's time to get your head out of the clouds and face reality. Not many small business owners will ever have the kind of money it takes to pay for an entire company holiday. In fact, many would have a hard time finding the resources and time to take their *own* cruise. I knew a business owner, years ago, that thought he was rich because he made a big sale and had more than £40,000 in his bank account. He ignored the fact that he owed his supplier more than £35,000 for the cost of the sale. I watched him spend more than £10,000 on personal and home items, and yes, he did go on a cruise. When his supplier's bill became due, he didn't have enough to pay it and wasn't able to purchase from them in the future. I saw him do this with other suppliers, and eventually his business went belly-up. It was easily avoidable and should never have happened. But when you can't control spending, the snowball gets bigger and bigger until it's too big to handle.

Don't back yourself into a corner with unnecessary spending and think that future sales will bail you out. You may not be able to process those future orders if suppliers stop shipping because of unpaid bills. You will not only lose the sale and the profit, but a valuable customer as well. Pay your suppliers first so you can stay in business and continue to use them.

Do You Really Need That Fancy Office?

We'd all like to live and work in luxury, but is it practical? A leather couch and TV in everyone's office, especially if bought on credit, can be a big hit on a small company's expense statement. Even if your business is doing great and you want to provide some extras for your employees, there's always a better use for the money. If you must buy fancy office and leisure furniture, put it in the break room only. Everyone will get to enjoy it there. What about exotic plants and a large fish tank? Put them in your reception area where employees and guests can enjoy them. But remember, with any quantity of plants, you need a maintenance service to take care of them. That's another semi-fixed expense if you sign a year or more contract. These are all fixed expenses you can't eliminate easily.

When business slows down, how will you pay for all these things? Will you have to lay off an employee to pay for your plant maintenance? It sounds a little ridiculous, but what are you going to do if funds are low and you're locked into a contract? If you want a fancy office, buy the little extras when you have excess cash and your other bills are paid. Always pay in full so you won't have payments hanging over you when and if business slows down. And watch for sales on those non-essential things you want for your office.

Also, the money you spend on fancy window treatments, carpets, and special order wall paint could be put to better use in marketing. A pleasant, reasonable office and a dynamic direct mail programme may use the same dollars as unnecessary office perks. An attractive, pleasant, functional, and clean office will impress employees and guests as much as any extravagance. When customers visit an office that's too elaborate, they start thinking about what you're charging them. They will assume that the money to pay for all these fancy items comes from the profits that you're making from them, which could lead to new negotiations on price when they make another purchase.

Used Equipment

Whether you're buying equipment for your office, store, or factory, consider buying some of the lesser-used equipment second-hand, and the more important items new, just to save a few pounds. When we opened a retail ice cream shop, we purchased about 40 percent of the equipment second-hand and only the most-worked items new. Our big, three-door ice cream freezer was new because it got constant use and worked at very low temperatures. Things such as a general-duty refrigerator and sandwich bar were bought used, and we never had a problem with them. Most of the items in the customer areas were new to give a good impression. And by buying all the equipment from one restaurant supplier, we were able to get a good package deal price with a few extras thrown in.

Factory equipment, printing presses, assembly line rollers, and other common items can all be purchased used or reconditioned. Just be sure that you get them with a guarantee in case something goes wrong. The only case in which you can't get a warranty is if you buy equipment at a bankruptcy or repossession sale. But prices may be so low that you can afford service if necessary. If the equipment is specialised or large, take an expert along to check it out before you purchase.

Some other equipment that you can consider buying used or refurbished is:

- Break room tables and chairs.
- Break room refrigerator and microwave.
- Employee lockers.
- Warehouse desks and chairs.
- Storage cabinets.
- General filing cabinets.
- Factory tables and packaging equipment.
- Fork lift trucks and accessories.
- Local delivery trucks.
- Restaurant sinks and fixtures.
- Maintenance equipment.
- Manufacturing machines if checked out.
- Clocks, pictures, and accessories.

- Back room restaurant accessories.
- Off-line equipment.
- Low volume copier.

Computers

This is one area in which I don't suggest buying used. Computer technology is changing so quickly that the computer you bought yesterday is becoming obsolete today. Most companies only use computers for accounting, processing orders, and to manage a website. It's also a great 24 hour global communication method using email. So why are businesses spending exorbitant amounts of money on the most up-to-date computer equipment? Email works on the older models, and so does the accounting program. You don't need to buy upgrades every time software and programs go from version 5.2 to 5.3. If you're in the computer software or security business, that's another story. It then becomes a cost-of-sales expense. But the rest of us can probably go for three to five years before we need to upgrade or purchase new computers.

Some small business owners feel they must have the newest and latest of everything in the computer world. They spend money on anything, whether or not it will benefit their business. If it came out today, they want it in their business tomorrow, at whatever cost. This is a waste of valuable resources that could be put to good use elsewhere. I can understand that many people are computer fanatics and love all the bells and whistles, but do it on your home computer. If computers are your hobby, that's great, and your non-business time and money is what you should use.

Another disadvantage of adding too many accessories is that your staff must be trained to use them. This takes valuable time that could be used for other things, such as marketing. And once employees learn all the new gadgets, how often will they use them? If they don't use them often, how will they remember the procedures? It's better to stay with the basic business equipment and software that will make your company successful.

Luxury Cars

We all love expensive cars. Small business owners can usually have a business car (check with your accountant for details) that the company pays for. It can be purchased or leased and billed monthly. A van, people mover or midsize car is the most desirable, and won't usually put the company in a financial bind. But if you think that because you own the company you can have any expensive car you want, the next question to ask yourself is, "Is it a smart thing to do?" Probably not, because you're adding a large fixed expense if it's not paid for in cash. If business gets slow and cash flow is sluggish, you still have that substantial payment due every month.

The BMW, Mercedes, and Lexus are all great car brands that most of us would love to have in our garage. That's the perfect place for it—in your garage at home and paid for with personal funds. This also ensures that you will keep the car should anything ever happen to the business. The car should be in your name, not the company's name. If you should need to apply for a bank loan and they question a large monthly expense, you have to come clean about the luxury car. Your average banker won't think you're choosing your expenses wisely.

Big Spaces

You all want to plan for growth and should have an optimistic outlook about your business. But you need to be prudent about the size of space you commit yourself to. Whether it is office space, a shop, or a factory, the rent or mortgage payment is due each month. Unless you're able to buy your space outright, and most small business owners can't, you're adding a fixed expense to your monthly statement. So when business is good, bad, or in between, that fixed expense is due. Be sure you can handle it during the tough times, because you'll have to.

If you're using a space that's currently bigger than you need, the extra money you're paying is not going to help your bottom line. In fact, it's reducing your bottom line by the amount you are paying for the space you're not using. Make sense? In other words, you're losing money on unused space until you grow into it, if you ever do.

What I've done with several companies in the past is to negotiate a two-year lease with an option to renew the same space at the end of the lease. I would also ask for an option to break the lease at any time if I lease a larger space (30 percent larger or more) that the landlord or management company handles. They will usually agree to this because they know that as you grow, you'll still be paying rent to them. By having this option, you can pay for only the space you need today, and you're not trapped if you outgrow it before the end of your lease.

If you're buying a building and it's bigger than you need now, but it's just what you want for the future, here's an idea: partition off a section that you don't currently plan to use and rent it out on a short-term lease, such as one to two years. You then get the space back and can expand into it or rent it out again. The rent helps pay the mortgage while your company is growing. The company that rents from you may also be a new or growing business. Another option, a couple of years down the road, is to sell the building to your renter and go find a bigger one. Then the process starts all over again. I have a friend who's in the nail and construction supply business who has done this several times. The rent and the profit on the sales have paid a large chunk toward the large building he now owns. I think I helped him move three times, and believe me, nail boxes are heavy! I hope he stays where he is for a while.

Unnecessary Personnel

When business slows down, you'll probably have people on your staff you really don't need. If you keep them there, it will be a drain on your cash flow and add expenses you don't need. So you must do something to reduce this outflow of valuable cash. Most owners hate to let anyone go, especially if they have been with you for a while and do a good job. But you have to think of the health of the business first, because without it, no one has a job. So sacrifices needs to be made, and you, the owner, must decide where.

Before you open the door and point, stop and plan what you really need to do. Figure out how many total hours you need to cut, and see if you can accomplish it by taking a few hours from a lot of employees. This may be hard to do if they're not paid hourly. You can also hold a meeting and explain the situation to all employees as a group. Then ask for any volunteers to take extended time off and be called back when things pick up. You might be surprised when one or two come forward that want to spend some time at home with their families, take a long trip, or take some college courses.

Also, be on the lookout for people you think may soon be leaving the company on their own. There's nothing worse than laying off good people, then having one of the remaining ones decide to leave. Listen and see if you hear grumblings coming from someone. Sit down with them and ask if they are planning to leave the company before you lay off someone else. Most people will admit their intentions and let you save someone else's job. Offer to write the person leaving a reference, if he or she is worthy of it. He or she can carry this along for future endeavours, and will remember you as always being honest. You never know, he or she might end up in a position where they can be a customer of yours.

So, you must find a way to reduce your staff and payroll that's the least painful for all concerned. It has to be done and *you* have to do it. Most of your employees will understand and realise you have no choice if you want the company to survive. And there's always a chance that the ones you let go will eventually work for your competitors. It's not a pretty picture, but you don't have another choice. Letting people go or temporarily laying them off is always a difficult task for any business owner.

You may also want to remind your employees that certain information is considered confidential and doesn't leave the company. This could be the information that would hamper your recovery and give unfair advantage to a competitor. Let your exiting employee(s) know that you appreciate their past work, and under other circumstances, you wouldn't want them to leave. You can ask each of them privately before they leave if you should call them back if business improves. The answer you get will give you an indication of how honest and loyal they will be when they leave. You can also enquire as to who would be available if you get surges in sales and need more people on a temporary basis. You can explain that they shouldn't just sit around and wait for you to call, but look for another position right away. Then if your turnaround takes longer than you expected or doesn't happen at all, you will have a clear conscience.

Employee Ordering

If you allow employees to place orders for store or warehouse stock, you need to review this procedure. They may be just ordering as usual when you should be cutting back or timing shipments to arrive just when you need them, not before. "But we always did it that way" is not acceptable when you're going through tough times. You have to fine-tune your ordering procedures so that your accounts payable invoices are spread out as much as possible. You might even want to

75

approve all purchases more than a certain amount so that you'll be able to check on its urgency. Don't make large purchases before you absolutely need them, because those invoices will come before they really have to. If cash flow is slow, you need as much time to pay as possible. Don't put your company in an even tighter position. Take the controls or at least set a policy on larger purchases.

What else are your employees ordering? Cases of soft drink, coffee, crisps, and other items for the break room? Is the employee refrigerator full of items you paid for but can't make you a profit? You may want to change the policy during slow times. Either eliminate these perks or set a budget such that employees can have one or two items and a spending cap. Anything else can be bought by all of them pitching in and buying it together. You might need to remind them that you're trying to save jobs by cutting unnecessary expenses. Getting a company back on its feet takes a shared effort from everyone. When the business is going well again, you can tell them you'll throw a party to celebrate.

Also, if big ticket items need to be purchased and it's an employee's job to select the make, model, and so on, he or she should know that you are the final approval. Let's say your copier breaks down and it's less expensive to buy a new one than to repair a much older one. Your employees will want the top-of-the-range with all the extras, but do you really need it? The midsize model will handle your needs nicely and save you a few thousand pounds. Don't let these purchases happen without your final review and approval. And if these are office, store, or factory equipment purchases that can be postponed, let your buyer wait until it's absolutely necessary. Keep an eye out for all non-essentials and catch them before your employee signs on the dotted line.

CHAPTER 7

Owner Neglect

Are you getting tired of the day-in, day-out routine of your business? Do you feel that some days you just want to walk out and let it run by itself? You've worked nine-12-hour days, six or seven days a week, and that's enough. The business is holding its own in the marketplace and you don't care if it grows anymore. Your growth record throughout the last few years has been good, so why push it? You've gone through good and bad times and now it's stable. You don't want to close it because you need the income; you just want to disappear for a while.

If this sounds a little far-fetched and ridiculous, don't laugh. I've seen it happen several times in my many years of knowing small business owners. They didn't realise that the years of growth and stability were happening because *they* were there. Take away the key ingredient and the cake won't rise any more, or at least not as much. Once they realise that their neglect has caused major problems, they try to jump back in and solve everything again. Sometimes they succeed, but other times, it's too late. The streetwise business owner knows that something needs to be done. When the business hit bumps in the road, they weren't there to do the steering and avoid the flat tyres. They may have ignored the problems they saw creeping up from a distance and weren't there to stop them before they got out of hand. Owner neglect can destroy a business that took years to become established and profitable. It takes years of the same owner's equity that made it all happen. They have earned a break, but can they really afford to take it? Let's take a look at some of the things that can happen when owners neglect their business.

Employees Slacking Off

When a business owner is not present at the business for long periods of time, things start to change. Employees stop looking over their shoulder to see if the boss is watching. Without adequate top-level supervision and direction, productivity and attitude can start to slip. There will, of course, be some shining stars that will perform at or above their expected level. But your average employee will stop doing the little extras that were so important in the company's long growth. Why? Because there's no one from the top to see them do it; recognition for a job well done will be gone. So why should they do more than the job calls for? There's no acknowledgement or words of appreciation for doing even an acceptable job. They get paid the same either way. There's little self satisfaction because it's not their company and probably never will be.

So, little things will begin to show up or not happen: the end-of-day clean-up will be less clean, or shelves will not be completely stocked; processing an order that came in late in the day will wait until tomorrow; people will begin to show up five minutes late instead of five minutes early; your five-star customer service will slip to three stars and a few complaints will start to creep in. But if the owner isn't there to hear the complaints or deal with them, why should the employees worry? Attitudes will change, and it may be too much trouble to help a customer with a non-routine purchase. They might just tell them you don't stock it anymore rather than go out of their way as they once did.

Employees may start to get into petty arguments with each other and refuse to work together as a team. If you have a supervisor, he or she may either turn into a dictator or a person that subordinates no longer listen to. All this internal strife comes across the counter or the phone for your customers and prospects to experience. An owner who is neglecting his or her business may hear of these grumblings and choose to ignore them. This will give the employees involved a clear go-ahead because no one is going to do anything about the problems. These are the times when other serious zero-tolerance problems can pop up. Situations such as sexual harassment, stealing, or fighting with customers can destroy a company quickly. If the owner isn't around to stop or deal with these situations, they can get way out of hand. Financial losses, lawsuits, and loss of many customers will build up fast. The overall business will begin to go downhill faster than a kid sliding down a banister.

Employees can make or break a company, as we all know. If an owner is going to be away from the store or office for extended periods of time, he or she needs to have a way to communicate. Give a few of the more trusted employees a mobile number where you can be reached. Don't disappear completely and let your business flounder without your input. Your employees will have to make decisions they weren't trained to make, and your many years of experience in the business won't come into play. Keep a line of communication open if you're going to be away, and call in periodically to find out what's happening. Ignoring the daily problems that businesses have can undo many years of past success.

If you see sales numbers starting to fall and can't seem to put your finger on the reason, it's time to check on your employees. Either call in at your place of business more often, or unexpectedly, to observe the actions and attitudes of your associates. Remind them that the health of the company *and* their jobs depends on their performance. Stress the point that they should be doing their job with care and diligence whether you're there or not. Drop a hint that you'll be stopping by unannounced from time to time, and make sure you follow through on it. If you can't find enough time to be there as much as you really want or need to, try using a mystery shopper.

The Benefits of a Mystery Shopper

Do you want to see how well you're doing against your competitor? Or how well you're doing compared to your expectations? Or what's going on when you're not there? Many times during your day-to-day routine, you overlook what's really going on at the front line. People who shop with you may not offer comments, complaints, or suggestions because it's too much effort, and they don't want to be labelled a troublemaker. So how do you find out this valuable information that is critical to improving your business?

To get the most objective information and opinions, you need someone who has no internal interest in your business. Someone who will "tell it like it is", whether it is good or bad. Actually, the negative information they can offer will help you much more than anything positive, although the positive information will tell you what not to change and to reinforce it if possible.

You have two choices of who to use to gather this information. You can hire a professional firm that specialises in mystery shopping and get a big stack of reports for an expensive fee. Most of the big corporations do this regularly and analyse the data in complex computer programs. This is great if you can afford it, and it will probably tell you things that you never thought of. But if you can't or don't want to pay the high fee, take the other option of finding your own shoppers. They can be people who have no vested interest in your business, or people who are familiar with your industry or type of business. You may also be able to find them through your chamber of commerce or other business organisations. Be on the lookout for them all the time, and don't hesitate to ask for their help when you find them.

Make a list of things you want them to look for, and leave space for other comments that aren't included on your list. A professional shopping firm will have their own agenda, but should also ask you what else you want to add. Once you've selected your person or persons, don't set specific times and dates; let them investigate on their own and report back to you when finished. Encourage them to be objective and give you the real facts. You're looking for things to improve, not fluffy compliments. As I said earlier, you can't change things for the better if you don't know about them.

When you get your mystery shoppers started at your shop or shops, why stop there? You can use these same people to visit your competitor's shops. Sam Walton, the founder of ASDA's parent company Wal-Mart, did this constantly, even to the point of being asked to leave. If you can't stand not knowing what your competitors are doing, get someone in there and find out. And don't be surprised if you find out they are also checking you out. When you get the reports and data for your stores and your competitors, look for areas where you can beat the competitors, and ways to stop any flaws in your operation. Don't wait around with your head in the clouds and a *high and mighty* attitude. There's always someone out there trying to take your customers; don't make it too easy for them.

You'll also find out if being away from your business has been costing you sales. If your results show that you need to be there more, then you will need to adjust your schedule. You can't just neglect a business that's not working well without you. If your interests have changed and you don't want to participate in the business anymore, you can make one of two decisions: either sell it, or turn it over to a family member to run. But don't let it falter just because you don't have the time or have lost interest.

Shrinkage and Theft

When an owner is not always around his or her small business, things start to disappear. It happens slowly at first, then if the disappearing goes unnoticed or disregarded, the losses start to accelerate. The cash register may be a little short, or cash has been taken out for questionable expenses. It seems that your customer level is about the same, but cash receipts are lower by 5 to 10 percent. How can this be? If you don't put a stop to little amounts, they start to get out of hand before you know it. Don't overlook small amounts in daily receipts, especially if losses are happening several times in a week; this is probably not a coincidence and should be investigated. If you're not even checking your daily receipts and cash to see if it balances out, then you need a way to do it, soon.

The person who makes out your daily report and counts the money should forward a copy to you every day. It can be via fax, phone, or email, but the owner needs to recognise any discrepancies daily, before they mount up. Any shortage of cash should be investigated right away to find the cause.

In more than 30 years of many different small businesses, I never really had this problem—at least not that I know of. Throughout the years, I developed a way to analyse people's honesty during an interview. I never cheated or stole from anyone, especially customers, even when I knew I could. So I didn't want anyone in my company doing it to me. Little things give away a dishonest person, and I can see it jump right out. Those types didn't last very long and, I'm sorry to say, probably went on to do it to someone else. If you feel you have a dishonest person on your staff, don't wait, do something about it. Dishonesty and stealing are like viruses—hard to cure, but they must be isolated. Unfortunately, large companies have so many employees that they tolerate a small percentage of stealing rather than trying to eliminate it. But a small business owner can't afford to tolerate any, and needs to act strongly and quickly when it's found.

Shrinkage, or internal inventory loss, is another money loser for a small business. If you, the owner, are not going to monitor inventory personally, there must be a system in place to keep track of it. Everything coming in the back door must be immediately logged into the inventory records on a computer. And everything going out the front door should be deducted from the inventory. What's left is what you have in stock and should be checked often, especially big ticket items. Owners of businesses did this manually for many years before computers, so it should be simple now with today's technology. It seems hard to believe that small business computers have only been around for 20 years. There's no excuse for a business owner not to know computer basics because it only takes about a two-week course to learn them.

Don't let disappearing inventory and cash ruin your business, and let everyone know there are no second chances if caught. A zero tolerance policy should be explained and posted in the employee break room. Have a reward programme for those reporting incidents; if they don't want to be known, have a way that they can report it anonymously. An owner can't see what's going on if he or she is not there, but others will be aware. We would all like to think we have honest employees, but it's that one-half of 1 percent that keeps us on the lookout.

The Slow Times

If your business has cycles of busy and slow months or periods, is this the time to stay away? Sure, it's a good time for holidays and trips, but it can also be the time to cut back expenses. When a business is small, the owner can pitch in and even reduce the hours of some part-time people. Many times in my business with less than five employees, I would be the one who remained at the end of the day during slow periods. I answered the few calls that came in and got firsthand exposure to callers' questions. I was able to see what employees were getting enquiries about.

Slow periods are good times to analyse past performance and see if changes need to be made. It's also a good time to look at reducing inventory and building it up again just before your busy period. It's not the time to forget about your business and stay away because it gets you down. Take this opportunity to look for new products to sell during this period. If every year it is slow in the summer, try to find something new that sells best during that time, or test several things and see what works best for your type of company. Then next year, it may not be as slow in the summer, and you'll have a chance to make extra profits. So you really have two choices for slow periods: either run away and hide until it's over, or do something about finding additional sales and profits. Obviously, the second choice is the correct one. Finding things that sell during slow times will add to cash flow rather than drain from it. You might just get lucky and find a new direction your company can pursue.

In our plastic card business, the summer months were the slowest times of the year and I was always on the lookout for a compatible product to promote during that time. We came across the idea of scratch-off game cards that restaurants and fast food places would buy or order in the summer for autumn promotions. At the time of writing, we're getting a lot of response from a direct mailing that went to more than 5,000 food establishments with three or more locations. Although we are getting new business this year, we hope it will really increase next summer with a little advance planning. So I think I'll hang around during the summer and monitor the results. It looks as though it will turn into a year-round product that fits nicely with our other products.

Should You Get a Partner?

I learned early in my entrepreneurial career that a partner is not for me. Why? Because, to me, it's like having a boss looking over your shoulder and questioning everything you do. In my first business, I had a partner who was not as gung-ho as I was, and was content with a lower level of success. I had a new family and wanted to build our company quickly, and hopefully make lots of money. We would always butt heads about spending money for marketing and books to enhance our business skills. We were doing okay, but I wanted more, faster. Eventually, we broke the company into parts and went our separate ways. He's still doing well today, and has a smaller company that he is very content with. He just didn't have the drive to own a big company the way I did, but that isn't necessarily a bad thing. He didn't take some of the risks I did, so he didn't experience all the ups and downs.

Now, after 30-plus years in many small businesses, I may be re-thinking the partner concept in certain situations. Friends who become business partners usually put a lot of stress on the friendship after a year or two. Usually, the more dominant person tries to be the leader, but runs into brick walls because of the other partner. If two or more partners can have separate responsibilities, and it's *written down* that the others can't overrule them, I think partnerships can work. The one assigned to the marketing function should be the more aggressive one and be given a budget to work with. No one else should criticise his or her decisions and he or she should be given free rein to market and grow the company.

Another situation in which a partner can play a big role is when the original owner wants to pursue other interests. You may not want to sell the company outright because you still need the income until your new endeavour takes off. You can bring in a partner to run the every-day activities of the current business while you are away more often. Part of the agreement with the new partner could be full ownership after a year or two when you, the original owner, want to completely get out. This way the person who is now running the business will have a financial interest in it. He or she will be more attentive and profit-oriented than just a manager you left in charge. So if you're getting tired of the business and want to phase out, a partner can be a great way to do it. You will need to spend some time with the new partner in order to train him or her in the way the business is currently operating; always be available by phone or email for any and all questions that come up unexpectedly.

CHAPTER 8
Bad Publicity

Publicity is great when it's positive, free, and helps promote your company. It can quickly get a company out of a sales slump or kick off a new product. Getting publicity should be a part of every marketing plan, especially for a small business. It can bring a little-known company into the limelight, and create an opportunity that money just can't buy. It can take a fledgling company into profitability with lightning speed, or old, established companies can double sales overnight with the right press release. Publicity is taken seriously because it's usually the opinion of the press, which is normally impartial and unbiased. The media is not going to give you a free advertisement; they want something newsworthy. So if it has news value and there's space or airtime available, you may get lucky. You want all the publicity you can get.

You obviously want anything positive that puts your business in front of your market. But what about the negative? What negative? You would never submit anything negative to the media. You don't have to; they find it or are tipped off by an informer. Most reporters have people out there in their specific field, digging up news. And when they get a tip and verify its accuracy, they're on it like a lion after a deer. It seems, sometimes, that they write first and ask questions later, which is not the best thing when it's your company that's being reported on.

Reporters at Your Door

You may drive up to your shop, factory, or office and see a few people lurking around like they're waiting for someone. Well guess what? That person may be you, and you have no idea why. So, what do you do? Escape as fast as you can and avoid the confrontation? Do you know if it is going to be a confrontation? If you don't know what it's all about, you need to find out right away. It's best to meet the media head on and see what it's all about.

Damage Control

If reporters start asking questions at a rapid-fire pace, there must be a serious problem, and you can't avoid it. If they start asking about a situation that you know nothing about, say so, but don't use the "no comment" reply. Let them know you're concerned, but that this is the first you've heard of the situation. You can't honestly answer their questions because you don't know the facts. If you do know of the problem but don't have a planned response, you'll need more time to reply. In either case, if you're caught off guard, don't stumble through a barrage of questions and give incriminating answers by mistake. Request some time to respond to their questions or accusations, so you can plan your answers. Ask for about two hours to study the problem and then you'll meet with them again. Any longer and they probably won't be able to wait and may submit a one-sided story. You certainly don't want that because you don't know what they know and where they got their information. So you want to have your chance to respond and have your side of the story included. Don't let them go public without you.

As soon as you've bought your two hours, get to work inside your company and find out what's going on. Whether the story involves your products, an employee, or yourself, you have less than two hours to get the real facts. Talk to all persons concerned and call your lawyer if necessary. You'll have to give a response and you need all the input you can get. If you're overwhelmed by the situation and you don't know how to respond, you need to bring your lawyer into the picture. Some lawyers won't want you to offer any comments, but you need to respond. Depending on how serious the situation is, you can just offer a statement. But being honest and showing concern is what's needed in circumstances like these.

Is It True?

Now, most bad publicity situations won't be as serious as previously described, but even a small bit of negative media exposure can be damaging. Don't ignore it, or it can expand or blow up before you realise it. The first thing you need to know is all the information concerning the adverse comments. What are they saying about your business, and is the story consistent from different sources? Review the allegations with some of your staff and decide whether it's all true. If it's not true, can you offer evidence to prove otherwise? Is it just hearsay from a dissatisfied customer? What facts does the media have to show it's true? Do they have real facts or just someone's accusations? How credible is the person or persons supplying the information? You don't want to brush off unreliable sources because the media has already accepted them.

If the situation is true or partially true, offer to take some type of action in order to correct it. If you can't give specific details of the solution, tell the media when you will have some plan of action. Don't offer a time that's too far in advance, or the press will think you're not taking the problem seriously. It's more to your advantage to come up with an action or solution as soon as possible, so it can be forgotten. The media won't forget and will keep bringing it up until you respond positively.

The best course to take is dealing with the public first to get your business out of the negative spotlight. Then look internally to find out what happened, why it happened, and how to avoid anything similar in the future. If a problem such as this one occurs in the near future, the damage will be much greater than the first time. Meet with everyone concerned and let them know how these situations can harm the company and their jobs.

When the Media Calls

Sometimes the first contact from the media on a negative situation will be by phone. Because you didn't know they were going to call, you or your staff may not be properly prepared.

You still need to have a basic plan in place to handle these types of calls. You may never need to use it, but if you do, it can save a lot of distress later. Instruct an operator, receptionist, or anyone who might answer the phone to connect the media only to a few select people. Don't give the call to just anyone who might give the incorrect response. Let only pre-warned employees or officers handle these calls. You'll want to have a meeting with all of them to discuss how to handle a surprise call such as this. You probably have a better chance of winning the lottery than having *Watchdog* or *Panorama* call, but it could happen to anyone at any time. These prime time programmes will definitely have some hard facts before they even attempt to make contact. There are actually companies in business to train executives how to handle news magazine shows. You can forget about hiring them because the cost is probably more than your total annual sales. But if you know any large company executives, you might ask if they were given any tips on how to handle big-time media.

Your first reaction may be fear, or to strike back defensively, but try to avoid either. Remember, the media are just doing their jobs and are after the story. The fact that you're part of the story means nothing to them, and if you're involved in the story, then you're their target.

Phrases *Not* to Use With the Media

When talking to the media, you must think before you speak. Because once it comes out of your mouth, they've got it. Be very selective on how you say things and don't speak too fast. Here are a few phrases that are better left unsaid:

- It's not our fault.
- We're only human.
- We're sorry, but...
- We don't have time for this.
- We can't be responsible.
- Humans make mistakes.
- We're busy, call tomorrow.
- Don't make me laugh.
- We're 99 percent innocent.
- I was out of town when it happened.
- We're not going to do anything.
- We can't be bothered with this.
- No comment (assumes guilt).
- Why should we care?

- Our competitors are doing it.
- It's how we run our business.
- Nobody's perfect.
- The public will forget.
- We'll look into it later.
- Just forget it; I did.
- Go chase a real story.
- I refuse to cooperate.
- We can't watch everyone.
- Submit your questions in writing.

What to Say When You Talk to the Media

Whether in person or on the phone, you will need to spend some time with reporters in response to anything negative. When they ask a question about a problem, you must not admit guilt at the offset. Be concerned, and offer solutions or actions you will take if needed. Admitting guilt before you know all the facts can be an unwise thing to do. Once you plead guilty and later find that it's not your company's fault, it's too late. Everyone will remember your guilty plea, and new facts won't change their minds. Don't offer to fix a problem even before you find out whose fault it is.

Request that all questions and answers be taped when you are with the media. This ensures that you are not misquoted, and that comments out of context are not used. If one of your answers is aired or printed and it's not what you said, you will quickly have to ask that it be corrected. You will always have the tape to refer back to. If possible, get a copy of the tape and keep it in a safe place. You never know when you might have to refer back to it. Things can come up in the future, and this will be your permanent proof of what you said.

Nothing is "off the record", so don't think just because you say it is, that's it. Reporters after a story will use everything they can sink their teeth into. Remember, they're not there to be your friend, they want the story. And the more negative the better, because it sells. Don't say anything you don't want printed or broadcast, because it probably will be. Even if you turn the recorder off, the reporter will have other means of recording.

Can you make it look as though you're the victim? Someone outside your company may be spreading rumours, whether true or untrue. Obviously, the first thing you think of is a competitor or sacked employee. But it could also be an unhappy customer or current employee. Regardless of who it is, is he or she revealing a truth or a fallacy? Is it something that you tried to sweep under the carpet, or just an absolute lie? Remember, things that you reveal to an employee can come back to haunt you later. If business gets slow and you need to cut back on employees or hours, there may be some resentment, and things you told them in confidence may come out. It's a normal human reaction to try and strike back. So be careful what you say and to whom you say it, because the future is difficult to predict—and this goes for distant family members as well. Many businesses have been destroyed because of disgruntled family members that have revealed company problems to the media.

How Long Will All of This Last?

Negative publicity will last as long as it's news and there's public interest. When the media has a story that *sells*, they will keep using it and adding to it as long as they can. They will keep digging for new facts and angles until the story is resolved or the public loses interest. This doesn't mean only on a national level, but may only be on a local level, which may be your target market. The media will do follow-ups to report the progress or the restitution of a problem.

I remember a restaurant a few years back that was temporarily closed because the health department found dead rodents in the kitchen. Everyone that enjoyed going there wondered how this could happen. I went there at least once a week for lunch and occasionally after work for a drink and free snacks. I couldn't help but think, "What was I eating?" This was a major owner error and was plastered on the front of the local papers and even in the big regional daily paper.

The restaurant was ordered to completely clean and disinfect the entire restaurant and have another inspection before it could reopen. The owner didn't panic, but was very concerned about the future of the restaurant. He had planned to do some work in the near future because the building had been there for about 20 years. Now was the time to do it and open with a clean slate. He closed for about a month and did a thorough upgrade to his kitchen and some of the customer seating areas. His new kitchen was so clean and modern that you could eat off the floor—well, okay, not quite. He bought big ads in the local papers to announce the grand reopening and invited the media with all their cameras and video equipment to a pre-opening party. He also offered all customers a supervised visit to the kitchen at any time to see how their food was being prepared and to check the cleanliness. At the reopening, after the new *positive* publicity, there was actually a wait for a table during lunch and dinner hours.

This is the way to turn a negative into a positive, and it took only about six weeks. Without this smart idea of renovating now, his business could have suffered for six months or more. He moved up a project he was going to do anyway and made it pay off. Assuming he also learned a valuable lesson, this situation should never happen again. From what I've seen since, business has increased about 30 to 50 percent over what it was before the negative publicity.

CHAPTER 9

Massive Competition

The old adage, "If you can't stand the heat, get out of the kitchen", says it all about competition. Don't think that if yours is a business, you'll have all the customers to yourself. You'll quickly learn the lesson of supply and demand, and, sometimes, over-supply and too little demand. You must learn to live with and prosper in the face of competition. Actually, your opposition can help increase sales and profits in some cases. That's why many similar shops are in the same area. The small shops hope the larger ones will bring in the people who will likely shop at several alternative places before they leave. The rent is higher, but the increased traffic near your business is usually worth it. The smaller shops prosper when people who have never heard of them find them there.

Commerce was built on competition throughout the years. When someone came out with a new widget, there was always someone working on the *improved* widget, then the *new improved widget*, then the *revolutionary* one, and so on. There is always someone working on a better way to do everything and steal the market, until the next *better* way comes along, and it always does eventually. One thing you can be sure of is that progress will happen, whether you want it to or not. Look at how the car evolved throughout the years and is still changing now. You can't stop innovation and the competition it creates; it's just going to happen. And even if you don't want to see it, your business will likely prosper from it as well. When you have to move over for something new, it's time to start looking for your better way. And there always is a better way or better product to be found. If you don't find it, someone else will. Then it will also force you to improve if you want to survive. Seldom do things stay the same for a decade or more.

While you're worried about all your competitors taking your business away, they are feeling the same about you. Your business is *their* competition, and everyone else's too. So, don't think you're the only one who is watching the other guy; they are watching you also. It may not always look that way because they are out there selling with confidence and not looking too worried. Show your concern *away* from your customers and do your offensive planning behind the scenes. When you have something new, keep it quiet until it's ready, tested, and available. As in poker, don't show your hand until you have to. The element of surprise will give you a chance to have the market all to yourself for a short time. I say a short time because your competitors won't roll over and play dead. They will try to retaliate and outdo you as fast as they can. So don't sit back with your feet up while the sales are pouring in, but look for an even better way or new product. You'll probably need it in the near future.

Back to Basics

If you have a lot of ideas you want to try for your business, that's a good thing. But going in too many directions at one time can also hurt the core of your business. This is where competitors can steal customers while you're not looking. You must keep an eye on your main business because that's the one that pays most of the bills and your payroll. When you feel your competition closing in, get back to the basics of your business and keep it strong. Don't take regular customers for granted, because someone is always trying to lure them away. And if you're more interested in new endeavours, you're leaving the door unlocked for those customers to be taken. You wouldn't leave your car unattended with the keys in it, so don't leave your customers unattended, either. The profit thieves are always lurking around.

Being a strong core company will be your best defence against those money-hungry competitors out there. They will always strike where the resistance is the weakest, and you should do the same. An aggressive move by a competitor should bring out the best in you and your business strategy. Keep looking for ways to improve your basic business and never accept the status quo for very long. If you fell asleep for 10 years, you would have a hard time recognising your type of business when you woke up. Sixteen years ago, there was no widespread internet, and a web was where a spider lived. Things can change quickly, and if you're not part of it, you're left behind. Your basic business needs to keep up with the changing times to stay profitable. So if you're in the mousetrap business, don't go off trying to sell luxury doghouses and assume no one will build a better mousetrap. By the time you find out it's happened, you'll have a tough time playing catch-up. And catch-up is more difficult and less profitable than being the leader, or at least close to the top; stay on top of your industry and move with it.

Think about the basics of your business and how you can improve on them. Small changes will work better than huge changes, and customers are more receptive to new ideas if the transition is easy. With big radical changes in your basic business, you have to re-educate customers, and some may not be willing to accept it. Always be looking to improve before your competition, but don't confuse customers just to be innovative. Look to other industries and see if you can apply their new ideas to your business. Keep it changing, keep it simple, and keep your customers coming back. Keep enhancing the basics in your industry as new ideas come along.

The Giant Discounter

This is probably the most asked question I get from small business owners: "ABC Discount Store is opening, how can I compete with them?" Or, "I can't compete on price with them, they are selling lower than my cost!" And, they are correct; they can't compete with them on price. They can't play their price game and win; the big stores won't let them. So what do you do? You don't play *their game*, you play *your game*.

Don't think everyone buys based on price, because they don't. How do I know that? Well, there would be no high quality clothing shops, jewellers, or fine dining restaurants, and certainly no luxury penthouse apartments for £1 million. People buy on *value*. Price is only relative to what you're receiving for it. If you're selling televisions or toothpaste off a metal shelf with concrete floors in a warehouse environment, the consumer expects to buy at the lowest price. But change that overall environment, demonstrate the product or service, and add knowledgeable service personnel, and the same product is worth more. Consumers recognise this, and price is not their first consideration anymore. They are buying an image of what you've created as a higher value.

Did you ever go into a giant discount superstore and not know exactly what you want or need and where in the store to find it? You feel as though you're in a foreign country and everyone speaks a different language. You know it's in the store somewhere, but where? And if you have questions about what you need or how to use it, it's like being in the desert looking for an oasis. There are probably people that can help, but where are they and how do you find them? You finally locate an employee, but he or she says it's not their department and he or she will call someone. He or she will tell you to go stand in aisle 14 and they will send someone over to help you. About 30 seconds later, you hear on the PA system, "customer in the blue shirt needs assistance in aisle 14",

While you're waiting in aisle 14, several other shoppers pass by and notice you're the one with the blue shirt. They assume you're an uninformed shopper who can't figure out where anything is. After four or five minutes when no one shows up, you decide to go back to the person who called for help and have them try something else. When you get back to where they were, of course, they're gone. So you look for another person and start the whole thing over again. When you finally get someone who can help you, they say it's out of stock or they don't carry what you need. There goes 30 minutes of your time and you haven't completed the task you started out to do. This happens many times every day in the big stores.

Is this what you're afraid of? Is a company with this type of customer experience going to steal all your business? I don't think so, unless you're treating your customers the same way. And if you are, as a small business, you should be worried. If you were the only one in your selling area offering certain products, you may have become too comfortable. You may have moved service to the bottom of the list because you didn't want to put in the effort. Now with competition coming in— big competition—you need a quick attitude change. You are no longer the only option a customer has; you're just one of the options. If a customer is going to be treated poorly or with indifference, they might as well go for the lowest price. Wouldn't you?

You need to raise the level of *value*, well above what the giant discount vendor offers. Then you must get the word out to let everyone know about it *before* your new competition is open for business in your selling area. Here are some ideas and things to consider, so you can prosper with a giant competitor in your selling area:

- A large discount store will draw more customers to your selling area from a farther distance. Your prospect base will soon double or triple. You can then be more selective about your target customers, and the products and services you sell to them.

- A large store takes six months or more to open, so you have plenty of time to plan your strategy. Don't wait until the last minute to change your selling style and add more value to your business. Start early and have a good foothold in your selective market.

- Establish a new brand awareness for your company. Project unique advantages for customers who purchase from you. Your brand is your name, products, or unique services. Offer something that no one else is offering and is hard to copy.

- Offer free delivery or installation, or a discount if the customers can pick it up themselves. Be on time with deliveries or offer a gift or premium if you are more than a half hour late. Have pleasant and well-groomed delivery personnel.

- Offer quantity discounts and free items with loyalty cards for regular customers. The big discount stores give no preference to frequent customers or large purchases. Show customers that you are aware of and appreciate their repeat business and referrals.

- Offer enhanced services or products, which can be sold at higher prices. Many people want convenience or top-of-the-line products, and the price is less important. Use terms such as silver, gold, platinum, premium, superior, executive, or premier to describe the higher level.

- Offer free car parking for customers who need special attention. Many elderly or disabled persons will show their loyalty for this service and pass the word to others.

- Train employees to become experts on your company's

products and services. You won't find this too often in the large stores. Have regular meetings or classes to keep your staff informed on new products. Have in-store monitors that show and demonstrate the latest products. Everyone likes to buy from an expert and will keep coming back.

- Try to visit your new competitor's store to find out what they're *not doing*. It's even worth a trip out of town or to another part of the country to see in advance what you will be up against when they arrive. You should easily find services that you can provide at a higher level and with more personal attention.

- Get out in the shop(s), meet your customers, and find out what improvements they would like to see. If you're selling to businesses, visit or call your regulars and ask the same questions. Everyone likes to talk to the owner who thanks them for their business.

- Extend your hours to accommodate the different buying habits of your customers and prospects. Make it convenient for them to shop or call when they aren't working or tied up doing other things. Remember, your objective is to accommodate *them*, not yourself.

- Call or visit other shops or offices in your industry that aren't direct competitors, and ask how they're coping with giant competition. You may get some ideas that you hadn't thought of. Let them know your door is open if they ever get into your town.

- Develop a network of other smaller businesses in your selling area and work together to keep the customers you have and acquire new ones that the big company will draw. Five or 10 people working together will come up with more ideas than just one person.

- Create a mailing list of your regular customers and send them special offers and announcements often. Keep them informed of industry changes and new products as soon as they occur. You can also start a one-page, two-sided newsletter with articles and facts about your industry and coming innovations.

- Find speciality products that complement your current business and aren't found in the bigger stores. Promote these items to special interest groups who may become customers because of the hard-to-find products. The word will get around and you'll be known as the only place in town to get certain, specific items.

- Make a shop within a shop and have a certain group of items that go together all in one place. You can use movable partitions to close off the area from the rest of the shop. When people walk in, they will feel like they've entered a different shop.

- Hold classes and how-to sessions on your products and services. Invite everyone and make it free. You can have outside guests come in to give the classes or do it yourself. Always tape some of the classes and lend the tapes to people who couldn't make the classes or prefer to learn at home.

- Bundle products that go together for a better deal for the customer and a bigger sale for you. It's like the lunch special at a deli such as a sandwich, crisps, and drink special is cheaper than buying all the items separately. This concept is also great for gifts or make-your-own gift baskets.

- Sponsor youth teams or fund-raising events in your general selling area. Always wear hats or shirts with your company name visible when volunteering. Either you or some of your staff should be in attendance at any events you sponsor. Let special interest groups know that your company is available to help in any fund-raising events.

The solution to competing with the giant stores and discount houses is to do something. Don't just sit there like a deer in headlights and wait for them to run over you, because they will. Be active and find things with which they can't compete. Price is probably not one of them, so let them be the lowest price. You want to be the best value, and let the buying public know it. Anyone can sell a tube of toothpaste for a penny more than the wholesale price, and people may buy it to clean their teeth. But if you have a speciality product that cleans your teeth, makes them whiter, keeps gums healthy, and also freshens your breath, its *value* will command a higher price.

So the secret to beating the bigger competitors, or at least holding your own business against them, is value. That's why customers will buy and continue to buy from you. Don't hide it— flaunt it, and make sure everyone knows about it. Keep improving the value you're offering by adding benefits, whenever possible. Many people will still shop at the big discount stores for some products, but when they want that enhanced service and higher value they will come knocking on your door if you're providing it. And you will be making a higher percentage profit on those speciality products.

Lots of Little Guys

There will be times when your competition won't only be the big discount stores, but also many other smaller businesses similar to yours. It may seem that every time you drive down the street, you see "Opening Soon" banners for shops in your field. It seems like a virus that keeps spreading. Most of the other businesses that are opening feel that there is enough business for everyone and *are* aware of your presence. If they've done the homework and checked the demographics, they can project the size of their target market. The fact is that they are not just going into business to steal your customers. They may have a new concept and see a few flaws in your business, but they could create or expand the current target market and bring new customers into the selling area. Be curious and find out about them by checking their websites if they have one or more shops in other places.

We opened our ice cream shop in a fast-growing family area of our city at a time when there wasn't another one within five miles. Ours was the scoop type, and had an old-fashioned family atmosphere. We also sold deli sandwiches, smoothies, and frozen yogurt. For about the first six months, we were king of the hill in our part of town. If you wanted ice cream, it was us or drive five miles. Even though we were without competition, we still provided excellent and friendly service in a clean environment. Then as new shops and malls popped up, we noticed another ice cream shop opening across the street nearby. This shop had a different concept of mixing the flavours and toppings into vanilla ice cream in front of the customer. We figured they weren't exactly a direct competitor and there were plenty of customers for both of us. And how could they serve a quality product if they made it in the back of the shop when ours was made with state-of-the-art equipment out of the area?

Another eight months passed and another (different name) ice cream shop opened about five miles away. Then another and another. We were now one of five shops inside that five-mile area where at one time we were the only one. We had to find a way to be unique and different from the rest. I started asking customers about the other shops and checked their websites to find out what they were missing. I found out that we were the only one selling frozen yogurt with half the calories of ice cream. Ours was all fat free, and one was also sugar free. We also had deli sandwiches with all fresh, sliced meat and cheese on bakery bread. The deli kept us in business during the colder months. So instead of promoting the ice cream, we concentrated on the frozen yogurt and sandwiches. We also offered free delivery during lunchtime to businesses in the area. Where else could you get a fresh milkshake or ice cream delivered? Although the business only grew a little each year, we were able to hold our own against all those new competitors. Time will tell if we survive and even more come into the area.

You need to find the different or unique product or service you can offer better than your competitors. The only way you can figure that out is to know their business and how it works. You can then promote why yours offers distinct and better products and services. If you're the only one in the area with a specific product or service, you need to get the word out. In all your advertising, mailings, and promotions, stress your unique product first. People may be looking for your unique product, and you need to tell them where to find it.

Learn to live with all your competitors, big and small. They are going to be there, you can count on it. Don't allow them to hurt your sales by sitting back instead of being proactive. Get in there and fight for your customers, and prosper instead of being defensive all the time. Don't let your competitors think that you fear them, and forge ahead with your marketing plans. And always try to offer something to your customers and prospects that is unique and different. The strong and confident will be the survivors, and size doesn't always matter.

CHAPTER 10
Excessive Salaries

Being in business for yourself can mean great financial rewards when you're doing well. Money should not be the main reason you started a business, but streetwise owners know money automatically comes with success. But when things slow down, you need to rethink your financial draw on the company. In most cases, the owner in a small business is the last one to be paid with what's left. You need to pay all your employees and bills, and put aside money for marketing your business first. Then a percentage of what's left can go in the owner's pocket. It doesn't really sound like much, does it? But in a growing, thriving business, it can be substantial. Sometimes, it can be much more than you dreamed of when you started the business.

Unfortunately, life has its ups and downs, and so will your business. Look what happened to the dot com companies at the turn of the century. Things were going so well for so long that even the pessimists thought it would never end. All expenses, including salaries, went sky high. Why? Because they had the money to pay for them, and it looked like a well that would never dry up. There was probably no plan to handle the decline that finally came. Owners and executives that were paid big salaries didn't consider taking cuts because they had so many personal commitments based on those big salaries. Big houses, luxury cars, boats, and high-limit credit cards were in style. So when the bubble eventually burst, their lifestyle plummeted.

While most small business owners will never see this type of roller-coaster ride, the volatile period will come. And if you're taking a salary that's most of the leftover profits, you will need the self-discipline to take a financial step back until things pick up again. I have made many excuses when my business slowed down, such as:

- "It will pick up next month."
- "It's the weather that slowed sales."
- "This economy is killing us."
- "Interest rates will soon fall."
- "We'll try some new marketing and sales will increase."
- "Our sales force needs a pep talk."
- "Every month can't be a record month."

These may all be true, but the reduced income needs to be compensated, for now. How can you pay the same salaries and expenses with less money coming in? The answer is that you can't—something has to give. Take it from someone who has made the mistake in the past—the situation will close in on you. And it can happen faster than you think.

So how do you avoid the owner-salary trap? Most people want to make as much as they can, don't they? With the owner's salary, a lower base should be set, which can be easily paid during slow and boom times. Then when there's even more money available to be paid as salary, one of two choices can be made:

1. The owner can take it as a quarterly bonus when the business is doing well.
2. It can be put in a mutual fund or money market account that the owner or the business can draw out of when needed.

Then, if the business slows down, the money is still there to pay fixed bills that never go away. I always preferred the mutual fund/money market idea because you can earn a little extra while waiting to dispense the money, although the quarterly bonus idea is great when you want to purchase a big ticket luxury.

Sure, you might think that the owner could take the big salary and just put the money back if needed. But once it's taken as salary, income taxes must be paid and 20 to 35 percent will be gone. Instead of having a little more money to use, there will be a lot less. Once you pay income taxes, you will want that money to be yours and not have to give it back. And what if you have already spent it? You can't take your new speedboat back to the dealer four months later and ask for a full refund. It's better to be sure the money is not needed before you pay yourself. And you should leave some behind as a cushion in case the unexpected happens. Don't think the unexpected never happens— that's why it's called the *unexpected.*

When there are partners involved such as a law firm, medical practice, or any type of partnership, they should share the obligation equally depending on percent of ownership. Salary increases and decreases should be in your partnership agreement right from the beginning. Thank goodness doctors and lawyers are excellent at their skills, but many times they lack the ability to run their business. This is why they should have a good business manager or staff to advise them of the total picture. Charging high fees doesn't always mean high profits unless the rest of the business is being run correctly. If the owner or owners are too busy or have no interest, they need a good watchdog to advise them. I've seen several times that a company looks busy, only to see them disappear shortly thereafter. You have to wonder how that can happen. But as busy as they seemed, more money was going out the back door than was coming in the front door. You need to know when this is happening and do something about it *quickly.* Base those big salaries on performance, and don't be too stubborn to reduce them when necessary. You must have the discipline to make the decision that will keep your business from a serious negative financial position.

Paying Employees

Most of us small business owners really like our employees. These people wake up every morning, shower, eat breakfast, and travel for 20 minutes or more to our business. They come in to work every day to do their job and help the company be successful and profitable. If they are doing their best to grow the company, shouldn't they share the rewards? Shouldn't they get a piece of the action when business is good? And my answer is *yes*, but to a certain degree. Most of us have been employees in the past, and felt we put in a pretty good effort. If you worked for a large company, you got reasonable benefits, but little else. The salary was satisfactory, but most large companies don't give bonuses to the rank and file. And praise for doing a good job—*what's that?*

A small business can offer many things that the larger companies don't bother with. A key employee should know that they are important by more than just their salary. You may want to pay them more than they can get elsewhere, but can the company really afford it? And unlike the owners' salaries, it's very difficult to reduce that salary when business is slow. So it's best not to overextend the company with excessive salaries to employees. Remember, you're all there to help grow the company, you need financial resources to do that, and salaries can drain a company's bank account rapidly. It's better to pay a good fair salary than to have to lay off people who are on high wages when times get tough.

For many employees, job security is just as important as a fair salary. What good is it to an employee to receive a high salary for nine months, only to have it cut off because the company can no longer afford him or her? This happens every day in large companies, and senior management thinks nothing of it. If you want to work for them, this is the risk you take. In fact, many small business people started their business because of the insecurity of big business. A smaller company can offer its best loyal employees a security you just don't find elsewhere. When you're raising a family, that regular wage comes in handy.

Paying employees fairly is the key to keeping them content and productive. Once they know that their salary is at least equal to that of others doing a similar job, there should be no resentment against the company. The way to find out about a fair salary is to check others in the same industry or job classification. You can check the job listings on many internet sites in your area of the country. Also, look at the type of company with the job listing and whether they are a large or small company. You want to use as close a comparison as possible.

I have also found other sites that don't list job openings, but they do list salary estimates for many different positions. I've also seen positions listed as entry level, junior, and senior level with a salary range for each. This is great information to help evaluate the people already on your staff. The best information to use is a compilation made from a survey of many different companies. Check to see how they get the information they use to determine the salary levels. You might also check with your chamber of commerce to see if they do a local salary survey. If they don't, you can suggest that they do, or even take charge of it yourself. Using several sources can give you the best idea of what others are paying their employees. Try searching "salary survey" on the web, and you should find several choices.

Arrivals and Departures

When it's time to add to your staff or replace a leaving or retiring employee, you always want the best person available. When and if you find that person, he or she may sometimes come with a high price tag. That price tag may be based on his or her own opinion or a past salary he or she received. There are a lot of considerations that should go into possibly hiring such people. A few of them are:

- Did they leave their last position voluntarily?
- If they were sacked, do you think the company was trying to eliminate their high salary?
- Do you think they would leave you if the grass looks greener on the other side?
- Can your business increase sales and/or profits by adding them?
- Will current employees demand raises if they find out what the new people are being paid?
- Do you feel they can be loyal to your business, or are they just out to enhance their personal ego?
- What will you do with them if you need to seriously cut back expenses?
- Will they run if they see financial problems arise?
- Can you keep them happy and challenged?
- Are they strong enough to take some of your business with them if they do decide to leave?
- Do you really need people of this ability, or are they overqualified for your company?
- How will you be able to refill their position if they ever do leave?
- Is this just an ego trip for you to have people of this calibre under your command?

Hiring employees is always a tricky and unsure situation in which money always comes into play for both parties. You must remember that it's your company's money and you must spend it wisely. It's better to start new employees at an average fair salary with early and frequent raises. I like to have preset raises at three months, six months, and at one year from the date of employment. After that, future increases will only come on merit, and you can explain how to receive them. This way, the new employee will know exactly what they will be paid a year from now, and can base his or her acceptance on that. These are only small increases while they are learning about the company, their job, and what's expected of them. If things aren't working out as planned for either party, the company has not overpaid them during the orientation period. You always have the option of accelerating those raises if you see that someone is really outstanding and contributing greatly to the company. But streetwise owners let time show the real value of a new recruit. There's an old saying: "Everyone is nice when you first meet them."

Then you'll have the quitters who will no longer want to be part of your business family. They will want to move on because they feel there is more opportunity and/or money elsewhere. Up until the time they actually give notice of leaving, you may hear little grumblings from them about not being paid enough or the fact that they are bored with their job. If you're lucky, they will ask for a meeting with you or their immediate superior and discuss their needs. If money comes up as a reason, you'll need to evaluate their real value to the company. Have you overlooked compensating them or are they asking for too much too fast? You'll need to make a decision because the meeting needs to have some conclusion. You don't want them infecting other employees with their comments.

You may also run into the unpleasant situation in which an employee offers you an ultimatum, such as, "Pay me X dollars or I'm leaving." This is an easy one for me: I immediately say goodbye and wish them luck. Never, never, never give in to an ultimatum; if the choice is pay or go, always choose go. The reason for letting them go without even thinking about it should be obvious—if it worked once, it will work again. And when your other employees hear about it (believe me they will) there will be a line outside your door that will scare you. I'd rather lose one good employee than ever give in to an ultimatum. You'll be a marked person and no one will ever forget it. I can't say it enough, let them go without question. I feel that any other decision puts the entire company in jeopardy. And even one employee, regardless of how good he or she is, is not worth it. You can put a sign on your desk like Harry Truman had, but yours will say "The ultimatum stops here."

Compensating Performance and Growth

When the business is doing well and there is some excess capital available, you may want to reward the people who helped you get there. The first thought may be, "let's give everyone a raise", That may be a great idea that all your employees would love, but let's think it over first. When you give out a raise, it's not temporary, it's permanent. You can't easily go back later and say that your business has slowed down and you need to rescind that raise you gave four months ago. Think about your employees' reaction. Not a pretty picture is it? How would you feel if it happened to you? Why not eliminate these tough-to-answer questions before they even come up? Rethink that raise in lieu of something better for the company's future. You won't have to make any undesirable decisions in the future.

Instead of a permanent raise, try a flat bonus that is paid once and is over with. No one expects a bonus every week, so doing it once gives you a little time before it's forgotten. A £100 bonus as a lump sum saves quite a bit over £10 a week for 52 weeks (£520). Plus, if you know that you have the money to pay the bonus now, you don't really know if you'll have the money to keep paying the raise nine months from now. If the company continues to do well, you can always declare another bonus in six months. But remind everyone that the bonuses are not automatic, and you need their help to keep the company's profit chart heading skyward. And of course, thank them for their past performance. A little praise makes the bonus money look even bigger and should put a smile on everyone's face.

And cash money is not the only option for a bonus. Most employees love paid time off. It's a good feeling to *not* work, but still be paid. But don't have more than one key person off at a time so the business can still run smoothly. Other things you can use to reward employees for good performance and company growth are:

- Personal gifts that they would value.
- Gift cards for great restaurants.
- Film or theatre tickets.

- In-house food and drink party.
- New TV or stereo for the break room.
- Drawing for a big vacation trip.
- Weekend trips to local hotels.
- Amusement park tickets.
- Gift cards for popular stores.
- Weekend car rental of a luxury model.
- Limo ride to and from work for a few days.
- Hard-to-get tickets to sports events.
- Bottle of expensive champagne or case of wine.
- Turkey for everyone at Christmas.
- Extra day's leave.
- Afternoon off for holiday shopping.
- Plaque for outstanding performance.

These are just a few ideas, and you can come up with a lot more. Or take a survey to find out what they really would like to receive as a bonus. You could make it multiple choice and give four or five options rather than getting too many other requests.

The one-time bonus or gift goes a long way in boosting morale. After the bonus wears off, your employees should want to make great efforts to achieve the next one. And the company is not locked in to something permanent that it would have difficulty paying later if sales and profits start slipping. You don't want to let someone go just to pay everyone else's raise. Because a small business can have unexpected peaks and valleys, you need to stay prepared at all times. Raises should be left to regular intervals as described when hiring and based on ability and merit.

Expensive Benefits

With the cost of health insurance and other benefits getting out of hand, it's difficult to give employees what you would really like to give them. As soon as available profits jump up to the next level, the cost of benefits follow closely behind. Large companies have so many people in their group policies that their rates per employee are much lower than a small business, so a smaller company needs to find a way to assist their employees without putting too much stress on its finances.

Other benefits such as car expenses and paying for classes and tuition can be decided on a case-by-case basis. I would suggest only paying for classes that will enhance their job performance and only if they get an A or B grade. You don't want to pay for someone else's cooking class (unless it's a bonus) and have them leave for a chef's position at a fine dining restaurant. That is not only a mistake, but it's embarrassing. I hate to be taken advantage of, especially when all the other employees know about it. So keep tuition refund benefits for knowledge you can use, and make them get your approval first.

Specify that any and all bonuses are at the discretion of management and based on company performance. You can always change something you've written down for the better, but it's not so easy to go the other way. Only guarantee what you're sure you can pay for, now *and* in the future. Because once it's on paper and in the employees' minds, they will fight to keep it. You don't want to terminate people or have them quit because of dissension over benefit issues.

So you can see that excessive salary issues mean more than just the owner's draw from the company, but it does start there and needs to be controlled there. Once small business owners realise that they just can't spend all the money on themselves before other obligations are taken care of, the stronger the company will be. And understanding that what you contribute to employee benefits and bonuses is safer if it's temporary rather than permanent, will let you sleep better at night. Don't be a scrooge, but don't be a spender either. Keep salaries and benefits at a manageable level that can withstand the normal ups and downs of the business.

Temporary Employees

Another way of controlling salaries and benefits is to use temps for those peak times of the year or when sales spike upward. Fast-growing sales make you wonder if it will last. Until you know the solid answer to that question, why add expenses that are difficult to get rid of later if sales fall back to previous levels? Why put yourself in a position where you have to dismiss someone you recently hired because you can't afford him or her? It's better to use a temp for easy-to-learn positions with no set guarantee of how long the position will last. And if business stays strong, most agencies have a temp-to-perm programme. The other advantage is that you can see how the temp performs his or her job before adding him or her to your permanent staff. Using temps is a good way to manage salary expenses when you're just not sure that business will remain at an elevated level. Find an agency and explain your needs, and if the agency provides the right type of people, stick with it for future needs. And let the temp person know your intentions.

CHAPTER 11

Major Order Error

We all love those big orders, don't we? The sales and profit numbers seem to make all the waiting worthwhile. Our employees are very excited, and so are we. You start to think about the other competitors that you beat out, but that's too bad, it's only business. Your company got the order and that's all that counts—today. The numbers start adding up in our minds even before we start to process the order. If we could get more of these, we'd be on easy street. You begin to think about how you were able to get this order, and use that strategy to get more like it. It wasn't so hard once you set your mind to it. This could open many doors for your business in the future; it's great! Now let's go after another one or two.

But wait a minute, you just received this big order; you haven't done anything with it yet. An order is not a sale until it's processed, delivered, accepted, and paid for. The customer's satisfaction plays a big part in making the order a final sale. In fact, the customer's satisfaction is *the* most important part of any order. Without it, the order and the sale are not really complete. And they won't be until you figure out how to make your customer content with his or her purchase. You have an obligation to process the order to the best of your company's ability. This is what the customer expects at the price you have agreed to. Getting the order is only the tip of the iceberg.

Early in my entrepreneurial career, I had a tendency to work hard to get many orders, especially substantial orders. It was a challenge to see if I was good enough to figure out how to beat the competition. Many times, the competition was the big guys that offered no personal service. Once I achieved the goal and the order was mine, I relaxed and went on to the next one. I forgot it was just an order and we had to follow through on it. All my effort was spent getting the order, not fulfilling it. I usually turned it over to an assistant who put the order into motion. The only problem was that because I had worked with the customer directly, I failed to specify a couple of changes they requested. As a result, the order was produced and delivered without the changes and the customer was ready to refuse it. We still had to pay for the cost, which would have been a big hit for our company, but we made a deal and lost all our profit and a little more because of it. After a couple of these situations, I paid more attention to detail and made sure that the order was done correctly.

I learned quickly after that about the value of following through on an order. A complete rejection could have almost forced us out of business. From then on, I made periodic checks on the larger orders to see that the customer's directions and requests were being followed. Whenever possible, we had the customer approve proofs or samples. Not doing so is just a disaster waiting to happen. Don't put the entire company on the line for one big order that should have been done correctly. Have a procedure in your business such that large orders don't move forward until several eyes have approved them. And one of these sets of eyes should be the person who initially worked with the customer.

Check and Sign Off on Each Step

When processing any type of large order, you need to follow it carefully. Whether it's being done in-house, or whether it is outsourced, precautions can be taken to be sure the product is exactly what the customer wants when it's shipped to them. This means giving special attention above and beyond your normal procedures. You can assign one or two people to follow each step and have a backup plan if one or both are not in for a day or two. You should have a separate and more thorough procedure for larger orders that will eliminate costly errors. You can also red flag the order form, job file, or paperwork for everyone on your staff to see.

The best safeguard is to have the customer review and approve each step themselves. If it's something that's going to be printed, a proof can be submitted, and all work would be put on hold until it's approved or changed. If it's a manufactured product, the customer can be invited to see the first few that are produced. A problem at this stage can be rectified before the entire order is done incorrectly. Make a notation on your production order or your purchase order that progress stops until approval is received at preset steps. Be sure that everyone involved is also told orally on these larger orders. If it's outsourced and your directions aren't followed, you should be off the hook for the cost of replacement, should the order be rejected. You should have a set procedure for large orders that all your employees know about. This protects you in the event of an order being placed when you're out of the office or out of town.

Who Takes the Blame?

Let's say your procedures were not followed, or you didn't have any because there were no problems in the past. But now there's a dilemma because the big order isn't exactly the way the customer requested on the purchase order. You could turn out the lights, lock the doors, and take the next plane to South America. That's still not going to solve the problem, so you might as well stay here and come up with some type of solution. Your future business, and maybe the entire company, depends on it. Running away from a major problem only makes it worse.

The first question will be, how did this happen? Who's responsible for the problem—you, your staff, or the customer? So before you panic, take all the paperwork concerning the order and go over it from start to finish. If the customer contacts you before you have time to review everything, tell him or her you're working on it as you speak. You will get back to him or her as fast as you can with more information. Don't accept any blame or try to blame the customer; you just don't have all the facts yet. Say that you understand that there is a problem and you'll be personally involved until it's solved.

Larger companies and corporations have a tendency to push their weight around and make immediate demands. Don't make any rash decisions or be pressured into giving answers until you have reviewed the entire situation. Give them a time when you will get back to them and make it long enough (but not too long) for you to be prepared. Most large companies take the assertive approach to make it look as though a problem could never be their fault. These people are usually protecting their jobs from reprimands by their superiors. Be very polite and cordial, but don't let them push you too fast with demands before you're ready. Once you say something, you may be held to it. Be courteous, but not too apologetic.

If, after reviewing everything, you find that the customer seems to be at fault by not specifying everything on the purchase order, you need to handle this carefully. You should call, fax, or email a detailed explanation of how the problem happened, and support it with the paperwork. Oral changes to a purchase order should always be followed by written confirmation. If this was not done, there's a fine line between right and wrong. You can't just say, "It's your fault", and that's it. If you want to save this order and ever do business with this customer again, you need to be empathetic. You may still have to make some concessions to keep the peace. You want to complete this order and get paid, so that should be your goal in any conversation or negotiation.

But what if you or your staff made the errors? Can you let this big order bring you to the brink of closing your business? People at your end still need to get paid. It will be very difficult to just toss this order aside and say that you'll just replace it with a new one. Most small companies don't have the resources to do this and stay solvent. You need a plan or compromise, and you need it quickly. You'll have to contact the customer, explain what happened and how it happened (if you know), and offer a solution. It's best to talk to everyone on your staff that was involved with the order to see where the problem originated. Blaming employees and chewing them out at this point is useless; you need to resolve the situation first. When you have one or two solutions in mind, it's time to call the customer.

Solving the Problem

Maybe *solving* is not the best word. *Bringing the problem to an end* may be more appropriate. You can't go on trying to figure out how it happened forever; it needs to come to an end. Otherwise, it will affect all your other business and orders. You need to work with the customer and come to a solution you both can live with. The sooner this is done, the sooner you can put this incident behind you. Because of the size of the order and the amount of money involved, you don't want to say you'll just replace it without some negotiation. So you want to ask some questions to find out what steps to take next:

- *Will the customer accept delivery?* If it's already been delivered and signed for by the customer, that adds a little to your bargaining power. It's already in their possession, not yours. The problem was obviously not found until it was unpacked and ready to use. Have they started to use it? Can you come up with a solution that will allow the customer to keep it?

- *Can it be fixed?* Is the problem with the order something that can be adjusted, corrected, mended, altered, or fixed in some way to make it acceptable? This is the least expensive way out in most cases if it can be done to the customer's satisfaction. Offer a plan stating what will be done and how long it will take to complete. Always get the customer's approval and commitment to accept it when the fixing process is finished. You don't want to spend money trying to correct the error and find out that they still won't accept it.

- *Can it be negotiated?* Is there a way for you to convince the customer to accept this order while you offer some restitution on their reorder or next order? Many times, the problem may just be an inconvenience, and making a future offer can resolve it. Think of what would pacify the customer now, make one or two offers, and let the customer choose. If he or she agrees, put it in writing and date it.

- *Can it be used at all?* Is there any way that the customer can use the order as it is now? If the answer is yes, you need to go back and negotiate some solution. Considering the financial loss that would be incurred by rejecting it, a deal needs to be made if it's usable. If you can't agree with the person who ordered it, look for another person in the company to negotiate with. Go as high up as necessary to get this done. There may be someone else of authority that is more sympathetic to your situation.

- *Will the customer accept a reduced price?* Probably the best negotiating tool when a problem occurs is money. A reduced price, special discount, free delivery, or longer payment terms can sometimes result in a solution. Don't make your biggest offer first, but start at a fair level. If you can only go as low as your cost, you've made a good deal. But even if the compromise can only be made if you take a small loss, it's better than replacing the entire order. Your profit margin may be low on a big order, so be careful how low you go.

- *Can it be sold to someone else?* If the order *as is* can be used by another one of your customers, that gives you another way out. Contact several of them and see if they are interested at this time. If the size of the order is too big, you can break it into parts to resell. You may have to lower the cost on this order so you can offer other customers a lower price than they usually pay to accept delivery now. You could also add free delivery or longer payment terms to make it worthwhile to them. This order needs to be paid for soon, so if someone else can use it, you need to make that deal now.

- *Can a competitor use it?* Is this type of product something that others in your industry can sell? This may be the last resort, but it's still a chance to salvage some of the loss. Making a deal with a competitor can be costly, but when you have few other choices, it's still an option. It's better to get out with less than take a chance of putting your company in a serious, negative financial position. So when your back is up against the wall, pick up the phone and make the call; you may be surprised at the response.

- *What if no one wants it?* Let's say you've exhausted all the previous options and still have no way to get part of your investment back. Another option, although not the best, is to contact a jobber, or someone who purchases overstocks and odd lots. They will probably be the lowest offer because they will try to sell it quickly at bargain basement prices. But when you get to this stage, some money back is better than none. Take what you can get and go on with your business.

- *Can it be sold at auction or at a bargain price on eBay or some other internet site?* There may be someone out there in the Web universe who is looking for what you have. It doesn't cost much to list it once and find out. You just might get lucky and sell it quickly, and maybe pick up a future customer at the same time. And selling it at an auction (even at a lower price) means you'll get paid up front.

Saving the Customer

When all is said and done, you have three objectives:

1. Get paid for this order and minimise the loss.
2. Keep the customer and get repeat orders.
3. Save face for the customer and your company.

Once you've accomplished number one, start thinking of whether this customer will ever order from you again. It may depend on how you handled the problem order and if there are any ill feelings on your customer's part. If you could tie in a bonus or special offer on the next order, to the solution of the order with the problem, you're more likely to get a future call. You want a chance to show that you can supply what the customer wants without any errors. And you want everyone involved to feel that the outcome was fair for both sides.

You need to consider the lifetime value of this customer, if there is one. A large company with a large order may be a one-time occurrence. The personnel may change, and it's hard to get much loyalty from a large company. If the order was received because of a low bid, then most of the other bidders will get to know the price. You may not even get the order at the same price next time; others may undercut you. Adding some value to the current order or making it unique will further your chances. One thing the customer should realise is that if there ever is a problem on an order, you will be there to take care of it when others may not.

Keeping the customer, if at all possible, should be in your mind when working on solving a problem order. If your product is unique or created especially for this customer, it will be a little easier. But if it's a generic stock item that can be purchased anywhere, you'll have a harder time. If you have provided good service to them in the past, you may have a better chance of continuing the relationship. But if the buyer has changed since the last order, you're not much better than your competitors. You'll have to build a rapport by the way you solve the problem.

Keeping them informed and returning all phone calls and emails will build confidence. If a problem order is handled quickly, fairly, and professionally, it can be a plus rather than a negative. Most buyers know that there will always be problems; it's how you handle them that really counts. But there may be a few cases in which the customer is so unreasonable that you don't want to take a chance on another order. In these rare situations, you must have the courage to walk away and chalk it all up to a learning experience. But you should put procedures in place to ensure that this type of problem never happens again.

CHAPTER 12

Lack of Business Knowledge

It doesn't really matter whether you run your business from home, a shop, or an office; the basics are the same. By the basics, I mean *business basics*—not your product or service. You might be the best mechanic, salesman, or chef, but without *business basics*, you open the door to possible failure. A business needs to be run like a business, not a hobby or a pastime. You can't spend 100 percent of your time serving customers and forget about the behind-the-scenes obligations. These responsibilities won't take care of themselves, and it is your duty to do them yourself, delegate, or outsource. The sooner you realise this, the better off you will be.

I've seen several businesses go through rocky times; some do not survive because the owner didn't know the basics of business. You don't need a business degree or masters in management or marketing, either. Most college courses that lead to degrees teach students how to work for a large corporation. A small business person needs to know more about being streetwise than how to put together a £2 million advertising campaign. That's why young people coming out of college need to start at a larger corporation until they decide what their real goals are. In a larger company, your job will focus on a specific area of the business, and you won't be responsible for the other areas. You may not even know how the other areas work. In a small business, your job as an owner will be the responsibility for all facets of the entire company, not just the area you enjoy. An owner wears many hats, and they all need to fit. You can't just overlook one area of the business because you have no interest in it. You're probably never going to enjoy 100 percent of your job, no matter what it is.

Most people that are starting a business for the first time don't know what it really takes to handle the business part of the business. Fortunately, your local library can offer a plethora of information, and all it costs you is time. Go see the reference librarian first and ask for the catalogue number of the subjects you need. Look in the reference section (you can't take these books out) and the general library section. Anything of importance that you can't remember from the reference department can be copied for about 10p a page. Take out books from the general library section and read up on the basics you lack. You don't have to be an expert in all areas of the business, but you do need to have some knowledge about them. There may also be DVDs or videos you can use or watch.

Some of the areas you want to have a fundamental understanding of are:

- *Bookkeeping/Accounting*—Learn how to read a financial statement, especially your own. Look at your cost-of-sales and expenses to see if any adjustments need to be made. Watch your cash flow and see if it is enough to pay your bills and invest in growth. Make sure your expenses aren't out of line for the profits you're making. The numbers say a lot, so know how to interpret them and keep them current.

- *Employee Relations/Hiring*—Read and learn how to energise and reward employees for the best productivity. Have meetings often and ask your people what they really want when business is good. You may be surprised that all the answers aren't money. Learn how to interview and hire new employees that will be an asset to your business. Know what questions you can't ask legally during an interview, and check references. Don't put up with moody or destructive behaviour, and don't be afraid to dismiss someone who is not performing up to your expectations.

- *Employment Laws*—There may be minimum age requirements and certain hours that students can work on school days. Also, find out about the minimum wage and when you have to pay overtime or any extra compensation. You also need to know if you or your employees need any type of personal licence to work at your business.

- *Advertising/Publicity*—A business owner needs to know what works for his or her type of business and industry. Picking the wrong advertising is a waste of valuable marketing funds. Find the best media that gives you the best results, and always test first before any long-term commitment. Ignoring free publicity is like winning a raffle and not taking your prize; study publicity strategies and make yourself available when publicity opportunities arise.

- *Direct Mail*—Almost every type of business can use direct mail in its marketing mix. Not knowing how and when to use it economically is passing up easy sales and profits. There are many books available that show you how to take advantage of direct mail on a tight budget. I've brought several businesses back to life by using mailings. Always stay in contact with your customers by regularly using mailings.

- *Computers/Websites*—Whether you're a computer wiz or not, you still need to know how to employ the technology for business purposes. Using email is now as common as the telephone and fax machine, and you must know the basics. Plus, almost every business needs to have its own website. It doesn't need to be very complex, but it's just as important as having a sign on your business door or building. You can easily find a website designer, and most of them are quick and inexpensive. Or take a class at college and do it yourself.

- *Customer Service/Complaints*—Great friendly service for your customers is no longer a bonus; it's expected. You may perceive that you're treating your patrons well, but it's what *they* think that really counts. Talk to them, use survey cards, and watch employees in action. Be aware of how you feel when you shop or buy from other businesses. There are many books on this subject in your library; read some and get ideas on how to improve service and increase loyalty. Great service should be a front-line policy for any small business, and handling customer complaints promptly and fairly can create goodwill.

- *Pricing/Competitors*—Your prices need to be competitive for the value you're offering. This doesn't mean you have to be the lowest price unless you're offering the lowest quality and no service. Your prices need to be in line with other businesses in your target marketplace. Be aware of your competitors and strive to provide customers with things your competitors are not. Running your business with your head in the sand will create a lot of headaches later and rivals will surpass you.

- *Repeat Business/Loyalty*—Repeat business can be the main factor that will keep you in business and help you recover from serious slow periods. You need to entice customers to return with special offers, frequent buyer perks, and preferred treatment. Your competitors are trying right now to steal your customers away, so don't just assume they are all automatically coming back to you. Loyalty is earned; it just doesn't happen by itself.

- *Negotiating*—When problems arise with customers, suppliers, lenders, and employees, you need to be able to negotiate solutions. Using demands to get your own way doesn't work very well in the business environment. You need to come up with solutions that satisfy both sides, not just yours. Special buying and selling situations will require you to make unique deals with customers and suppliers. A great deal can be profitable if done correctly.

- *Sales/Telemarketing*—Products and services don't sell themselves, even if they are the best in the market. You need to present your business to the people who are your most likely customers, and then remind them over and over again. If you don't like sales or telemarketing, then you need to hire employees who are trained and proficient in this area. But you can't forget about sales altogether, because part of being an owner is being an enthusiastic representative of your company 24/7.

- *Taxes/Licences*—Here are two things that need to be paid for *and* paid for on time. Your accountant and lawyer can deal with the paperwork, but it's your responsibility to get taxes paid on time. You can't tell the government that your accountant forgot to give you the paperwork; you still owe the penalty and interest. Getting too far behind on taxes can build a mountain that is impossible to climb over.

- *Trade Shows/Exhibiting and Attending*—Just about every industry has conventions and trade shows annually to inform and reveal the latest products and developments. If your type of business can afford to exhibit, it's worth a test to see if it's profitable. But even if you can't exhibit, you should attend at least one a year. This is the only way to keep abreast of competitors and offer the latest innovations available in your industry. Things are changing and improving constantly, and you might lose your market position if you have to play catch-up later.

These are some of the things you need to know a little about for your business to succeed. You can always delegate some of these areas to employees, but you, the owner, have the final responsibility. When someone in charge of one of these areas leaves your company, *you'd* better be ready to carry the ball until a new employee is in place. Once you have opened and operated your first business, you'll be streetwise in these areas for your next business.

Books, Tapes, and CDs

You don't need a degree, master's degree, or a high-priced tutor to learn the basics of business. But you do need the interest, desire, and a little time. And don't say you don't have the time, because you do, and I'll show you how. When you drive to work, to appointments, or to pick up supplies, you are spending time in your car. Many business books and speakers have tapes and CDs available just for that reason. Unless your local football team is on the radio, why not use that time to learn more about your business and reinforce what you already know? Buy them online at discounts or check your library to see what they have available.

Even if you don't go out for lunch, you probably eat at your desk or somewhere in your business. Instead of reading the newspaper (you can get quick news on the internet) or doing the crossword puzzle, why not have a business book ready to read? There are so many books available on almost any business subject that you'll probably never run out of available titles. I usually buy used books at a much lower cost, scan the chapters that give the most usable information, and put them on the bookshelf for future reference. I try to group books by subject so that if something comes up, I can quickly go to that section and get an answer or an idea. You don't have to read every word in every book; some areas don't apply to your business, and some of the information you already know.

By purchasing good-condition used or sale books, you can build a business library quickly. Tapes and CDs can also be purchased used or on clearance. Some of the best deals I've found are through Amazon.co.uk and Play.com. Even new books are discounted as much as 20 to 40 percent off the published price. You can also check the websites of unabridged audio book publishers, because many of their titles are not available elsewhere. They all have websites and catalogues that offer periodic sales. I check them all every 90 days or so to see what's new and available. More specialist business books are available from business publishers direct like www.pearsoned.co.uk/bookshop.

When you run out of new material to listen to or read, go back and repeat some of the best ones from before. You can't possibly remember everything you read or hear but you can remember the best books or tapes. Listen to or read them again and pick up some new ideas. I have about 20 favourite cassette and CD programmes that I try to review about every six to nine months. I enjoy listening to them again and always pick up new ideas or knowledge. They can provide inform- ation that you didn't need last year, but may pertain to your business now.

Colleges and Seminars

Your local college is a great source to learn all about running a business. Your local taxes support the college, so the cost of courses is lower than a university. You can select a subject that you need to know more about and forget the rest. It's not the qualifications you want, it's the information. When you look through their course circular, you'll also see short courses on specific business areas. They are designed to target one area if that's all you need to learn. In some cases, a local businessperson may be the instructor, so you'll receive hands-on training from someone with real experience. And real experience is your first choice instead of a textbook.

Another source of learning and ideas is the travelling seminar. They will be focused on certain parts of running a business and last one to three days. Bigger cities will get two or three visits a year. Most businesses will receive a flyer in the mail about four to six weeks in advance, and they usually require you to sign up early. If you don't get a mailing for the type of seminar you need, search the internet, and you're sure to find some. Just search by the subject followed by the word *seminar*. Of course there will be a cost, but it's well worth it if you need the information. A couple of hundred pounds for the seminar can save you or make you thousands later. It's an investment rather than an expense. And seminars zero in on the topic in depth, so you won't have to listen to subjects that don't interest you.

Learning about business in a class or seminar where there are other people opens even more doors than you expected. Most of the other attendees will be like you, owners or would-be owners, so when they ask questions, you'll get the benefit of hearing the answers they get. They may bring up some areas you hadn't thought of—but now you will know. So when you need to know things about running your business, sign up, attend, and get the answers.

Chambers and Business Groups

If you're new in business, new in town, or just tired of being a business loner, joining a group might be for you. Most business groups and chambers of commerce meet monthly and have a speaker or discussion group. This does not mean joining a leads group—that's for sales and usually doesn't provide business knowledge. The chamber members are normally owners, partners, or high-ranking executives of companies in the city or county. They talk about the business climate in the area and other matters that affect commerce in general. You may also find lawyers and accountants there that will discuss their expertise with you off the clock. Be sure to offer any ideas to them that you feel might be useful. Remember, everyone is there to pick up ideas, views, and opinions. It's a give and take situation, so participate.

If there's a meal at the meeting or function you're attending, try to select a seat with people you don't know or haven't met yet. And *please*, have a lot of crisp new business cards with you. Meeting new businesspeople in your area will be an asset you will value highly in the future. When you collect business cards from others, write a note on the back to help you remember something about them. It's hard to recall something about a person that you just met briefly. And if they don't remember you at first, your note about them may help refresh their memory. You may also need to contact one of your fellow members for quick advice when a serious problem pops up. The more people you know from groups, the more people you can rely on for help when it's needed.

Check Out the Government

Another source of help with your business knowledge is your friendly government. Some of the government's information may be a little dated, but a lot of it is free. They have many publications that you can purchase at a low cost on specific business areas. Before relying too much on any information, check the date when it was written. Most general information is good for years because it doesn't change that much. The best source of information is Business Link (www.businesslink.gov.uk) which offers specialist business advice in a range of areas as well as extra help and guidance for start-ups.

Consider a Partner or Mentor

If there are areas of running your business you just don't understand or have no interest in, then you need another person to help you. One choice is a partner who will have a serious interest in the business just like you do. A *partner* doesn't mean he or she will be equal unless you allow him or her to acquire at least 50 percent of it. A partner can own as little as 5 percent and still have an ownership interest in being a success. Sam Walton, the founder of Wal-Mart, did this with many of his early stores. He would let the store manager buy 5 to 10 percent of a new store, and he knew they would exert that extra effort to make it successful. Have you seen his company lately?

When searching for a partner, you want someone who has the business skills and knowledge that you are lacking. Then he or she can be responsible for those areas that you cannot handle or don't want to handle. This can take a burden off of you and let you concentrate on your own areas of expertise. Any partner should have the same goals for the business that you have to avoid problems in the future. This should all be discussed and put on paper before any deal is finalised. A partner can be a valuable addition to your company, but you don't want him or her to turn into an adversary later. Make sure you discuss in depth the responsibilities of your new partner and put it on paper. Both of you need to sign the agreement, keep a copy, and send a copy to your lawyers for safekeeping. If you're thinking of having more than one partner, I'd advise against it until you take the time to absorb one, which would be at least a year.

Another option is to work with a mentor or a coach to assist you in areas in which you are lacking expertise. The word *coach* means money, so be prepared to pay. There are many different types of coaches in business, so check them out carefully before obligating yourself and your company to any long-term contract. Be sure to call a few references that were seeking similar advice, and ask them if the coach was worth the money they paid and if they could use him or her again. Be careful of coaching organisations that charge up front or big monthly fees and only offer a few hours of on-site help. Try to get an escape clause put it into any contract so you have a way out if you're not completely satisfied and it's not helping you.

A mentor, on the other hand, may or may not be free. Many successful businesspeople really enjoy helping business owners and won't charge for their help and advice. An occasional lunch, dinner, or gift would probably be appreciated. Don't be too demanding; they are doing you a favour and can get along nicely without you if it's too much trouble. There may be a case in which a mentor will ask you for something in return for his or her time if the desired results are achieved. If your company is not currently profitable, but turns around with his or her help, you could offer a small percentage of the new profit, or a percentage of the increased profit, or just a flat fee. Mentors are great because they are not acting as a hired hand; they really want to help you succeed. Ask people you meet at chambers of commerce meetings if they are interested or know any other successful people you can contact.

Internet Sites and Newsletters

I've already mentioned the Business Link site, but there are many others with valuable information. You just need to search for what you're interested in learning. There are also colleges that offer courses on the Web that you don't have to attend in person until the end. If you're not able to spend the time in a classroom, do it at home or in the office. You can select only the business class you want, and learn at your leisure. This seems to be the new trend because people never find the time to drive to a college and sit in a class. Check out www.icslearn.co.uk and www.open.ac.uk for two of the most popular distance-learning sites.

Other business sites can be found if you search by subject, such as marketing, accounting, advertising, and so on. Just put the words *small business* in front of the subject and you'll zero in on sites that will have information for you. There's always some new idea, trend, or case study that you never thought of or can use immediately. Bookmark the sites you find most informative and visit them at least once a month for updates.

You can also visit the sites of your competitors to see what they are offering and what's new. If you have a website, they are probably checking it out to see what you're up to. By watching competitor websites often, you can react faster to changes and new products and services they may have recently added. You might even see prices for some of their products and decide whether you need to adjust yours.

There are several business newsletters you can subscribe to for the latest business and marketing ideas. Some are available on the internet, but be careful what you sign up for before you give out any personal information. Others come in the mail and can be great reading during a quick lunch. We also have one available for a low cost at www.idealetter.com. If you get just one idea out of each newsletter issue, it's well worth the subscription price. Most of them will be easily affordable; only renew the ones that provide information you can use. They should be a deductible business expense.

Get Out of Town

Another source of usable business information is other companies similar to yours, but not in your selling area or target market. Call several business owners from cities similar in size to yours but far enough

away so they are not competitors. Call them and explain that you would like to visit them and see how they run their business. When you get a couple that are willing to work with you, go and see them. This can be an invaluable experience, and you're sure to pick up many ideas, tips, and great information. You'll get to see a business similar to yours actually operating, and learn the things that make them successful. Be sure to bring a gift or buy the proprietors a great dinner to thank them.

Also, when you're out of town on a business trip, convention, or holiday, just stop in at a business similar to yours and ask for the owner. See if you can spend an hour with him or her and discuss ideas and solutions to problems. Leave with an open-door invitation to visit your business if he or she is ever in your town. You can always find an hour or two when you are on a trip, so don't waste it sitting in your room watching television. Get out and take advantage of an opportunity that may not come along again. You may learn some valuable streetwise information. Tap into every business resource you can find to gain useful knowledge.

CHAPTER 13
Obsolete Products and Services

The dictionary defines *obsolete* as out of date, old-fashioned, antiquated, and of less use. Does this sound similar to anything you're trying to sell? If you have become too comfortable with selling the same products and services, it's time to wake up and smell the market. Very few, if any, products last for decades without improvements or upgrades. Look at cars: they have been selling for a hundred years now, but how much of the original ones are in today's models? The concept is the same, but the structure changes regularly. In fact, most cars become out of date every five to 10 years, and companies offer changes in each year's models. When you see an older car, say 15 years old, driving on the street, don't you wonder who would ever buy one like that? Would a car dealer stay in business if he only sold 15-year-old looking cars, even if they were new?

Many business owners become too comfortable marketing what always sold well. You might think, "Why change when it's still doing well?" In part, they're right—for a while. But if you're running your business with blinkers on, you may get overtaken. Sure, you can keep offering the same products and services year after year until three things happen:

1. Major improvements in your product become available in the market.
2. Your competitors offer good alternative products and start making encroachments on your customer base.
3. The market for your products dies completely.

Some classic examples of obsolete products that would seriously harm your business if you didn't change are:

- *8-Track tapes*—there is a warehouse somewhere that has brand new ones stacked to the roof.
- *Black-and-white TVs*—Did you know you can still buy these?
- *Record player needles*—great for antique collectors, but no longer for the mass market.
- *Tyres with inner tubes*—what a pain this was when you got a flat.
- *Manual typewriters*—without electric, the speed is slow and it's difficult to correct mistakes.
- *Leisure suits*—unless you're going to a 1970s-themed party, they are out—but they may come back someday.
- *Summerhouses*—now here is something your guests will hate on those cold nights.
- *Flash cubes*—a great idea in it's time, but the built-in flash and other technology concealed their usefulness.
- *Manual pinsetters*—what bowler wants to wait until the guy at the back resets the rack?
- *Cut-throat razors*—barbers may still use them, but the consumers aren't buying.
- *Coal stoves*—that dumper truck with the load of coal is as hard to find as a winning lottery ticket.

Some of these may sound a little silly today, but they all were popular in their own time. Companies stopped selling them because people stopped buying them. Hopefully, they saw the change coming before it was too late, and were able to order the improved products along the way. Waiting until the last minute will require you to play catch-up and sometimes be left in the dust. So when you see changes coming in your products, services, and industry, don't fight it. It's going to go on with or without you.

Competition Breeds Change

Your family business may have created a product that was really outstanding in its time. The market for this product may have also grown throughout the years and business really started to climb.

Because you had a patent to make this product, you were king of the hill, and no one could touch you. The profits rolled in because you didn't have to be too price-conscious—there was no competition. If someone wanted the product, you were the source, period. Suppliers of raw materials, packaging, and waste removal grovelled at your feet for some part of the action. You could dictate your terms because volume was good and you were a continual buyer. You could work in the morning, delegate duties, and play golf in the afternoon. There was no reason for research or new product searches because you already had the best product or product line.

But slowly, behind your back, competition was working on a way to serve your market and chip away at your sales. They were working on another product to fill the same need or another way of offering a competing service. Your product or service may have been so good for it's time that it was difficult to knock you off the top. I said *difficult*, not impossible. In 1980, it was *impossible* to have a powerful computer that would sit on your desk. Isn't there an old saying, "A difficult task takes time, the impossible takes a little longer"? What's impossible at one time can become a reality later on, and many times it does. Remember, an unbeatable sports team only is such until beaten.

Competitors are always looking for ways to increase market share with new products and services. If your company is a success, your competitors want to take away some of that success with improvements or innovations. So if you are not also looking for ways to improve, those long-time big sellers may become obsolete. And once they are obsolete, it may be too late for a comeback. Your company and products may be labelled as old-fashioned and ineffective in the marketplace. And remember, your competitors aren't going to inform you about their progress in creating a *better mousetrap*. They are probably going to spring it on you, the market, and your customers all at once. They will likely plan their attack to take you by surprise and your first reaction will be awe and anxiety.

A great competitive product can make yours obsolete in a very short time, especially if you don't have a response ready quickly. Think about computers—as soon as a new faster chip is announced, who's buying the old, slower one anymore? Maybe your industry doesn't change this fast, but it will change. And if you're left standing there with your mouth open and a puzzled look on your face, your comeback will be difficult or impossible (remember that word?).

Technology Changes

In current times, your customers and target market don't *hope* for new technology, they *expect* it. They usually expect it from the leader in the industry, but that doesn't mean that they won't flock to a smaller company for new ideas. New technology doesn't have to be big, earth-shaking innovations. It can be small improvements and upgrades to products in smaller market segments. And new technology doesn't have to apply only to electronics; it can also be found in restaurants, dry cleaners, car washes, and beauty salons. Any type of business can offer new ideas that can improve an industry. So don't think that if you're not in the computer or communications business, you can't have serious money-making positive changes.

But if you are in a fast-changing industry, your products can be obsolete even faster. So it may be wise not to overstock an item that can become obsolete tomorrow. The hi-tech industry has no mercy for anyone who does not stay current with everything that's happening. You don't get an email or letter in the mail saying changes are here; you must stay in the loop somehow and find out yourself. Bringing positive changes and updates to your products or service can reinforce repeat business and lure in new customers. By offering the latest innovations in your industry, you can build a reason to do a mailing to your target market or offer new ideas in your advertising. It gives you a chance to show what's new and rekindle that interest in being your customer again. Car dealers do this every year when the new models come out, so check your post. And don't think they would do it year after year if it wasn't working.

New technology in any industry is not only exciting for the customer, but also for the seller. But remember, the customers don't care about the technology itself; they just want to know what it will do for them. It gives you a chance to learn something new and become an expert all over again. The buyers in your industry will eventually turn to the latest innovations, so if you are still trying to sell the old model, your sales chart will look like a ski jump. Stay up to date on all the new products by attending conventions and trade shows. You'll probably find new things for your business that will

amaze you. Don't be stuck with yesterday's model when others are selling tomorrow's.

Generation Changes

Every 25 years or so, a new generation moves into the buyer age. They may have new wants and needs in the products they buy. If you're trying to sell what always appealed to the previous generation, you're going to run into problems. The new generation may not want it, and if forced on them, they'll go elsewhere. What was once a hot item becomes obsolete quickly. Consider whether your father's idea of cool squares with your own. Thought not.

The same goes with clothes—the new generation doesn't want to look like their parents. They want their own individuality, and how they dress is what you see first. The manufacturers as well as the stores have to target their styles to the generation that will buy them. Styles change so quickly, especially for the younger generation, that stores reduce prices to get some of their cost back.

The new and upcoming generations can change markets rather quickly. They can put demands on an industry and will hold back until the product is what they want. If you ignore them and don't change to satisfy them, someone else will, and your sales will start slipping. And if you try to play catch-up later, it will be more difficult. By not trying to supply the new generation's wants and needs, you'll be known as the place *not* to shop. And once people get that in their minds, it's not easy to change them back. It's even harder if your competitors are supplying what they want, so don't wait for the cash register to stop ringing before you start catering to generation changes. A few years from now the new generation will probably be the main buying market segment where most of the sales will be made.

Poor Backup Service

When products become obsolete and are no longer big sellers—or even average sellers—the after-sales service begins to dwindle. Not many people want to provide backup service for products for which the business is shrinking. Think about where you would go for service on a vintage car. If you're still selling old products, you'd better be able to provide the service yourself or know someone who can. Once a generation passes, the new one is learning to service the hot current products. They have no knowledge or interest in the obsolete models.

And worse yet, what if a part is needed for an obsolete product? Do you know where to get it? What if it's out of stock? Does it cost more because it's hard to find? And even if you get a new part, let's go back to where to find someone who can do the replacement service. Many times, the original manufacturer will make an announcement that on a certain date in the future, they will not make or supply any more replacement parts for certain products. What do you tell an irate customer six months after selling them an obsolete product? Maybe you talked them into the older product because you offered a low price and needed to get rid of it fast. Now they want to know what you're going to do to help them because parts and service are no longer available. I suppose you could pack up and move to New Zealand before all the other buyers come knocking on your door.

Some of these examples may seem a little extreme, but if you're the customer, you want answers. How do you answer the question, "Why did you sell me this when you knew there might not be service available?" This is certainly one person you don't want out there giving negative word-of-mouth advertising. You'll quickly make a name for your business as the place from which *not* to buy. And don't think word doesn't travel fast in a marketplace. Some of your buyers may be members of the chamber of commerce or other local organisations. They have regular meetings and discuss what's going on in the area to help each other. There may even be an obsolete product buyer that will complain to your local Trading Standards. You don't want to be on record as having complaints against you.

Other Problems

Trying to sell products that are becoming obsolete can open other doors of aggravation. Because the owner and sales staff are not having contact with the latest innovations, their knowledge won't be up to par. When customers ask questions about new products they've heard about, how can you answer them? You don't have any experience or background to know the answer. In some cases, potential customers will shake their heads or roll their eyes as they head for the door. And you know where they are going—to your competitors of course. You had the first chance at their money, but you blew it; you probably won't get a second chance.

You will notice that sales figures keep slipping and your target market is shrinking. In fact, the market you sold to previously may be changing to accommodate the new products, and the market may break away and form its own doomed entity. You may eventually have that breakaway market all to yourself. The only problem is that there are few, if any, buyers in that market. It's like trying to sell lawnmowers in the desert; you may find one fool, but not many more. Your business will get a reputation for being old-fashioned and not up with current times.

In most cases, it's the business owner's fault for selling and being stuck with obsolete products. They enjoyed good sales and growth for a long time with the same products and got too comfortable and lazy. Meanwhile, competitors are doing all they can to be in on the changing market, and the more they see your business sitting idle, the more their enthusiasm builds. You see this a lot when a big discount store moves into a smaller market. Some owners of small businesses refuse to change and eventually disappear. Others consider it an opportunity to take advantage of the increased buying power that the big store brings to the area. So take a good look at your current product and service list and decide what's in and what's not.

CHAPTER 14

Ownership Change

Very few businesses keep the same owner(s) for a generation or more. Just as in the rest of your life, interests and goals change at times. Your wonderful business that you treated like a child, cared for, and helped grow, is now ready to go off on its own. Either it doesn't need you, or you don't need it anymore. Other interests are taking the place of that everyday challenge, so it's time for a new owner to step in.

But a new owner can be a shock to an established business. It's similar to a divorced parent remarrying and the only child has to get used to the new spouse all of a sudden. The intentions may be good, but there's a time of adjustment before things run smoothly. And that time of adjustment can vary in length for each different situation. In some cases, the adjustment period is short, and things get back to normal almost immediately. But in other cases, everything is dragged out, and it seems as though the adjustment period will never end.

Changing the ownership of a business can cause some real problems, and in some situations, can destroy it completely. Just as people are different from each other, so is the way they will operate the same business. Even small differences can change the way customers see the company, and it can alter their comfort level. This doesn't mean that it will always change for the worse, but any change is, well, change. There have been numerous cases in which a failing business has been sold and the new owners turned it around completely. But this chapter is about the opposite, when things go from good to bad or from bad to worse. I'm going to look at the reasons for the decline, and how to stop it before it's too late. Knowing what the actual problems are, is the first step toward correcting them.

A New Owner's First Month

If you are a new owner, or have recently sold your business to someone, I feel there are a couple of guidelines to follow right from the start. And this is especially important if the new owner still owes you money from the sale, and it will be paid over time. If he or she isn't successful, how is he or she going to pay you? And if he or she doesn't pay you, will you get a weakened business back? The best situation is to get off on the right foot *before* a remedy is needed.

From past experiences and observations, I feel that any new owner of any business should make *no* changes in the first and maybe second months. Leave things alone until you learn how the business has been running. There may be reasons for some of the things you want to change. But maybe some of those changes would improve the business. You won't really know the correct moves to make if you don't make an honest observation first. You may look foolish and waste a lot of time if you change something and have to change it back again. Have some patience, and learn and master the current system before you change it.

When the time has come to make the needed changes, don't go it alone. Two of the best sources of input and ideas are your employees and your customers. Most employees have ideas to improve your business, but they may not have been encouraged to offer them to the former owners. Let them know that you want to hear their views and opinions. Remember that many of them have been there a lot longer than you, and they have seen the business from different perspectives. If you like some of their ideas (and you will), offer some type of reward or bonus for the ones you use. Otherwise, why should they even bother to help you in the future?

The other great source for ideas—your customers—can also offer suggestions you never thought of. And why shouldn't you ask them and listen to them? You would have no business without them. They are the people who are handing you money for your products and services. Why not let them tell you what they want? Past owners may have become too comfortable (another term for *lazy*) with things as they were, and ignored customer requests and suggestions. And that's another good reason why a new owner can bring a business back to life. If customers' requests are disregarded, they may just go see your competitors to see if they listen. And if your competitors *do* pay attention and implement changes, your sales chart will be pointing toward Antarctica. A new owner has the chance to reverse this and possibly bring some of those customers back. Spend that early learning period paying attention to what your customers want and need, so that you can plan your strategy.

Listening, asking, and observing are the best approaches in the beginning. Don't jump in and stir up systems and procedures before you weigh the pros and cons. Don't take the chance of making a current rocky situation worse and drag the business down even more. Get all the input you can and look at all the possibilities prior to making any decisions.

Saving Money by Cutting Quality

A new owner can make a serious mistake by reducing quality and service to save money. I'm sure they think this saving will go right to the bottom line, but they're wrong. Reducing the quality of products that buyers are accustomed to will only harm the business, not save it. If you think that regular customers won't notice, you're sadly mistaken—they'll know right away. Some will make their dissatisfaction known to you; others you just won't see anymore. You are much better off increasing your prices a little and leaving the quality and service alone. It's much easier to explain a price increase than why you had to reduce the quality or service. There's a saying that I always think of: "Poor quality is long remembered after price is forgotten." Once a customer is comfortable (there's that word again) with a company's quality and price, they will usually keep buying. But make that eventual change of either and the boat starts to rock. However, it rocks a little less when the price changes, and it will soon become the regular price they expect.

Cutting quality and service to make more profit is only a short-term gain, and may be shorter than you think; don't fall into this trap. One alternative is to offer a new product or service that is lower in quality *and* at a reduced price. Don't change the long-term standard. The new choice will be for people who are willing to accept less to pay less. Talk to them about it and don't hide anything. They may have their own reasons why they will accept a lower quality to save money; give *them* the choice.

I am far from being a handyman, and I start to get a headache when I have to try to fix something or do a project around the house. My small collection of tools is so seldom used they look almost new. So when I had to go and buy a hammer (I can't find our old one), I didn't want to pay for the best model available. For the two or three times a year I use it, the basic model is good enough. However, a carpenter or craftsman who uses his hammer every day wants the best, and is willing to pay more for it. That's why when you go to a hardware store there are choices at different price levels. A new owner should expand those choices, not eliminate them. In fact, an even higher-quality product at a higher price may increase your profit, so look for ways to offer even more choices of quality and leave the current ones alone. You can't fool the customer because the joke will be on you.

Can't Handle the Stress?

Owning a small business is not for the timid and weak. If your life has been all fun and games, you're in for a shock when you step into your first business. When you visit other businesses, everything looks like it's running smoothly from the customer's viewpoint. That's the way it's supposed to look to the *outsider*. But go behind the scenes and spend a day with the owner or manager and you may need some aspirin. There's an entire other world there that most customers never see, and probably don't want to see. If you ever get invited into the kitchen of a busy restaurant on a Saturday night, you won't believe it. You'll never figure out how they get all the orders done correctly and in a timely fashion. In my opinion, a busy restaurant kitchen is either a work of art or a disaster. That's why most restaurant owners stay out of the kitchen and let the head chef run it.

When purchasing an existing business, there needs to be a certain amount of due diligence. But if you're only looking at the numbers on the financial reports, you're making a big mistake. There's a lot more to a business than what you see in the reports. In fact, the reports may be a little misleading if that's all you rely on. If I were making the purchase, I would get in the physical part of the business. Follow the owner or manager around for a day or two and see the good and bad aspects. Is this the type of business you really want to work at every day? Can you handle the stress level and problems that will come up? If you're easily flustered and ready to run out the door, then maybe you should look elsewhere for a calmer situation.

But if you can answer at least a qualified yes to these questions, then look at the reports. A thriving business will probably come with a big price tag. A business that is stagnant or slipping a little can be a better bargain if you think you can fix it. But fixing it will likely need a cash injection for marketing and other improvements. Are you financially and mentally prepared to do this? Or are you already in a tight position just trying to handle the purchase price? Only the potential owner can answer these questions because he or she will have to live with the stress.

New Owner Training

Unless you're walking into a business type that you ran before, you will need training. And don't think that it looks so easy you can pick it up in a week. When you buy a franchise, there's a preset programme to get you started. And usually there will also be some on-site supervision and consultants. But with an independent business, you're on your own, so you need to make training and long-term consultation part of the deal. The selling owners usually want to escape as soon as possible, but don't let them go too fast.

When making your training deal, the existing owner will try to end their on-site training in a week or 10 days. Try to get a little longer even if it's fewer hours per day. You'll be surprised how many situations come up that you didn't expect. Such as what the backup source is when a supplier can't deliver or items are out of stock? Or who do you call when equipment breaks down or the copier stops working? These things do happen, and they happen when you're least prepared. Even after the on-site training is over, try to negotiate a 60- to 90-day phone lifeline for unexpected situations. Some of the problems in a business only occur occasionally, and you need to find the solutions quickly.

Personnel Problems

Each owner's style of management will be different, and the employees will pick up on it right away. They will be comfortable and complacent doing their jobs just the same way they always have. Most people don't like change, especially if they don't have a choice about it.

145

Some may even rebel and insist on doing things the way the former owner let them, which is probably another good reason why a new owner should leave things as they are for the first month or so and learn the current system. Then discuss any planned changes with senior employees first and get their input. Once you have a feeling and feedback on your changes, call a general meeting with everyone and lay out your plan.

Any new changes should be made gradually, not all at once. Too much too soon can not only put stress on the employees, but on the customers as well. Give everyone, including yourself, some time to adjust step by step rather than by big leaps. This also gives you a chance to see how any changes are being accepted as they are implemented. If something is not working the way you anticipated, you can still reverse it before anything gets out of hand. And not making all the changes at one time will let you see how employees and customers are adjusting.

In most cases, your personnel will respond positively to changes that improve the business. After all, if the business is successful, they will be also. Once a series of changes is implemented and working well, employees will feel less stressed and more confident in their jobs. And I don't need to tell you that a relaxed and confident employee does a better job. When employees see the company performance improve, it will give them a greater feeling of job security.

Failing to Promote the Business

Some new owners may come into a business and don't want to spend any money on marketing or promotion. This can be a mistake because the previous owners, knowing that they were going to sell, may have cut way back on their spending. This can curtail bringing new customers into the business, which is what a different owner needs to make the investment pay off quickly. Before a new owner takes over, he or she should have a meeting with the current owner to find out what marketing methods were being used and what worked best. Some things might not have ever worked, and that knowledge can save the new owner some initial marketing money.

Every business needs some marketing and promotion. I don't care if it's been in business for 50 years, there's a different generation of customers that need to know about it. Word of mouth and past performance are great, but not enough. They don't reach everyone in your target market, and those potential customers won't buy from you. Isn't a new owner's objective to do better than the previous one and increase sales and profits? That's why people put money in a mutual fund—not to see the value stay the same, but to constantly increase. You want your business investment to prosper and be worth more through time. It needs marketing and promotion to move ahead, and a new owner has to invest the time and money.

Remember, you may lose some customers after an ownership change due to the fact that people don't like change. Some of these customer losses are a natural part of the transition, and you can't do anything about it. But what you can do is bring in two or three times the customers you have lost. Promotions that make special offers for first-time customers work well if promoted correctly. Check what your competitors are doing in the media and on their websites and compare it to what your company has not done. Don't spend all your time learning how to run the internal workings of your new endeavour, because there's much more to it. Promoting and marketing are an important part of taking over a business; don't ignore them.

Mistakes Lose Customers

I know you're going to say that everyone makes mistakes. Well, you're right, and it's how you handle them that really counts. But I'm not saying that honest little mistakes are going to lose customers; it's the big ones that should never happen. These mistakes occur when someone is not paying attention and not following general procedure. There are problems on orders that really inconvenience a customer or that happen more than once. These are things that a customer won't put up with and will find another source to buy from.

Let's say you own a cafe and deliver lunch orders to businesses in your selling area. Your delivery customers can either call in their orders or fax them to you. So on an order for five sandwiches, one person doesn't want mayonnaise and one doesn't want mustard. If the sandwiches are delivered without honouring those requests, the people ordering are obviously going to be upset. Also, if the delivery was late, they will have to eat quickly and get back to work. Can you see yourself on the receiving end of this? What are the chances you will want to order lunch from this cafe anytime soon?

It's more likely that these mistakes will happen when a new owner takes over because they don't have the long-term knowledge to eliminate them. New owners seem to be a magnet for these types of mistakes that can alienate customers. They should ask the previous owner about common mistakes for their type of business and how to catch them before they happen. And what do customers expect as restitution? To save a repeat customer, you need to act quickly and offer more than the problem caused them. New owners need to have a plan in mind so they will have fast solutions available. Long-term employees can also offer ideas of what worked in the past. A new owner should make a special effort to stop critical mistakes *before* they happen.

What Happens When the Owner Retires or Dies?

There comes a time for most people when we've had enough of working and building a business. If we're lucky, we can make this choice ourselves and actually plan for it. Planning for retirement should be a two to three year period in which the transition of the business should be gradual. Then you can see if things are actually progressing the way you intended. If not, you will still have time to stop and change course. Don't take the chance of having something that you spent years of your life building get destroyed when you leave. If you're like most business owners, you want to see your company go on and be prosperous.

For some owners, retirement can be a welcome relief and a door they've been waiting to open. But for others, they just can't seem to tear themselves away. Sometimes they even stay too long, and it harms the business because they are no longer injecting the new ideas that the business needs. When the business was new, *you were the business*, but as it matures, it develops the ability to survive without you. It's sort of like raising a child who will grow up and have a life of its own.

The next question after the *when* is the *who*. Who is going to follow in your footsteps and continue doing everything the way you did? The easy answer to that is *no one*. No one is going to run your business exactly the way you did. If you're not going to sell your business, the next alternative is to turn it over to a son, daughter, or other relative. Most owners feel that they can trust their family and still have a little control of their actions in the business. But this can also fail if the new owners decide to make radical changes too quickly. Young people today want results fast and may take chances their predecessor didn't. Most customers don't like changes that are too extreme, and may rebel by purchasing elsewhere, which is why an owner needs to transfer power slowly and stay involved along the way. Being open to change is good, but look at all the options before they are introduced. Don't take the chance of alienating any customers that are valuable to the future success of the business.

What if the unthinkable happens, such as a business owner passing away unexpectedly? Most of us don't even like to think of such a thing, so we don't. But even if it has only a tiny chance of happening, there is still a chance. Do you have a plan in place, or does the business go down with you? Some type of succession procedure should already be determined, and your key people should know about it. Even if there is no one available to take command, the business should go on as normally as possible until it can be sold. The company accountant and lawyer should be able to determine a fair value to sell the business quickly. You may be able to set up a power-of-attorney with your lawyer that only becomes effective in the event of your death. Don't let the business just waste away; have some sequence of action set up. Be prepared for the unexpected and save what you worked many years to build. After all, we do buy life insurance, don't we?

A Case Study in Progress

We sold our deli and ice cream shop after starting it from scratch and running it for more than three years. We were so tired of the long hours, especially in the summer, that we reduced the price so that it was a great deal. The first serious offer was $3,000 less than our asking price, but we took it to get out fast. I think we knew then that the lady and her son purchasing the business were not the right people to run the store, but we went ahead anyway. They had to be approved by the franchise main office, so we knew that the final decision would not be ours. So we moved ahead, crossed our fingers, and hoped they would be approved. The president of the franchise corporation knew how badly we wanted to get out so he gave his approval.

Part of the approval was a mandatory trip to the home office for training on reports and procedures. The new owner, her son, and her sister scheduled a trip for about 10 days later and spent three days of in-office training. This is when the red flag of problems started to come up. On the first day of training, the teenage son didn't even show up (he was going to be the manager of the store). The new owner, who was lacking a 100 percent command of the English language, and her sister attended the training, and seemed a little puzzled. The second day, the son showed up, but laid his head on the conference table and slept through most of the session. The third day, the son attended, but was playing a computer game at the table. The president of the franchise company walked in and told him that if he heard one more beep, he would break both the game and his finger. The training session was over, but did they really learn anything?

Also required was that a representative from the home office had to come to the store for on-site training after the deal was closed. Part of closing the deal was that we would pay the transfer fee and the expenses of that trip to the store for the representative. This was another £2,000 we agreed to. When the in-store training started, the son didn't show up for three days, and the new owner left to go shopping. Very little training was done, and it seemed like a waste of money for the trip. In their early days of ownership, they didn't know how to prepare a lot of the items on the menu, which frustrated customers. There were a couple of other delis and ice cream stores in the area, so the customers did have a choice. We were also on call for questions and assistance for the next three weeks. She certainly called with questions that should have been answered in training.

It was going into the time of year that this type of store should be doing well: warm, spring days when people and families went out for ice cream and frozen yoghurt. We always did our best business from March to September. We found out that after a couple of weeks, the son lost interest and stopped coming in to work at the store. We provided the names of several of our past good employees that she tried to hire. But after a few days, they left, saying they couldn't work for her or couldn't understand her. Service to customers was getting worse and she was running out of popular items. We knew that most of our old regular customers would be coming back because they didn't know we had sold the shop. But would they keep coming back again after their encounter with the new owner? Also, as a side note, she was not doing any advertising or promotions to attract new customers.

We also did lunchtime sandwich deliveries to companies in the area. We gave the new owner two mailing lists: one of lunchtime companies that order for delivery and another of more than 850 consumers that had signed up to receive flyers and coupons. The last time we asked, she did nothing with them and just threw them in a drawer. We also heard that deliveries to our regular customers were 30 to 60 minutes late, and some items were missing. Another disaster was when an order for 18 sandwiches was delivered on Tuesday, but the customer's fax said the meeting was on Thursday. An unhappy customer and a £50 food loss. These are just a few of the many mismanagement stories that seem to be happening constantly. After only three months, she is trying to sell the shop again because she knows it's not the correct business for her. I hate to see something that we spent more than three years building disappear. The shop is still open, though, so there's still hope that another owner will come along and save it.

CHAPTER 15
Collection Problems

For non-retail and non-cash businesses, collecting money due for products and services can sometimes be a challenge. Some business owners get a little lax for fear of upsetting a customer. Let's look at the situation from a different angle. If your customer is another business, and it buys your product to be used in its office, why should it use it *free* after the grace period? (The grace period, on your terms, could be 15, 20, or 30 days.) And if it is using your product to manufacture or enhance its own product, your product is making that business money. The people there can't expect you to let them have a *free ride* until they feel like paying, so don't let them. Collect what is owed to you in a businesslike manner.

Many large companies that have been in business for a long time may let customers take longer to pay their invoices because they aren't in a tight cash position. The cash flow is larger and has less day-to-day pressure. But a small business seems to always be short of cash and must collect its dues on time. In fact, you will often get behind on your own bills if your customers don't pay you on time. When you supply your products or services, don't your customers expect on-time delivery? Why should paying your invoice be any different? Don't hope that they will pay on time—expect it and do something if it's not done. I've never been bashful about asking for money after providing a quality product or service, and neither should you. If you want to stay in business without having your own financial problems, you must collect *your* money in a timely fashion. Let me say again that not doing so will eventually put your business in a short cash situation. And if you haven't experienced that yet, believe me, you won't like it. You'll spend a good chunk of your day searching for sources of money to pay your own bills and taking overdue calls. And remember that once the product or service is rendered, it's your money, not your customers'. It just happens to be in their bank account until you can get them to take it out and send it to you. And a lot of them will drag their feet if you let them, so don't. Be diligent in collecting payment for your invoices when they are due.

Ask for a Deposit

Here's one way to improve collections right up front. We have devised a way to get customers to pay in advance and feel it's just routine. In our plastic card business, we sell to associations and companies all across the country. Most of the orders are more than £500, and some go as high as £25,000. So we have a policy that on the first order or a repeat order more than two years later, we require a 50 percent deposit to start the order. New customers can pay this deposit using a debit or credit card. And in most cases, we trust them for the balance that is billed when the order (which takes two to four weeks) ships out. If we sense that they are bothered about giving a deposit to someone they never did business with before, we suggest using a credit card. They have the protection of being able to file a claim if the product is never delivered. But because of our professional product literature and the abundance of samples we send, we rarely have a problem receiving a deposit.

If the order is for a large amount, you can set up a partial payment schedule of one-third to start the order, one-third when it's ready to ship, and the balance billed with 20- or 30-day terms. This way, they will see some progress before the second payment is made. You could also show them a sample of the finished product to verify that it was done correctly. Trying to collect 100 percent of the price in advance will make many customers back off. How would you feel paying for a product or service in full before it's even started, especially if you've never done business with the company before? The one exception though is a previous customer who was difficult to collect from in the past. If you don't feel comfortable with a past customer paying for a new order on time, require another deposit or full payment in advance. You can't make a profit if the order is never paid for.

There will be cases when a large national company or organisation refuses to pay a deposit on an order. In most cases, what they will owe you will be a fraction of one percent of their expenditures, and it will be paid on time, or close to it. You need to make a decision of whether you want to accept their order on *their* terms. Even if you have a unique product, you probably won't get them to change their mind. We've run into this a few times with major casinos that absolutely refuse to pay any deposit, and will take their business elsewhere if forced to do so. We make a quick credit check on the Web and have processed their orders without a deposit. But if you're going to do this, make sure you have a valid, signed, written purchase order with a number on it and the payment terms specified. That purchase order number must be on your invoice and sent to the correct accounting department. And it also must be on all shipping paperwork for the delivery to be accepted. If you follow the correct procedures, you should be paid on time. But don't hesitate to make a follow-up phone call if you're not.

Once an order is received, processed, delivered, and paid for in a timely manner for a new customer, we don't require a deposit on subsequent orders. The one exception might be a large order that followed a smaller one. This policy can protect you from having someone place and pay quickly for a small order first, then drag out payment on a larger one. And don't think this doesn't happen, because I can verify it firsthand. It doesn't occur that often, but once is too much for me. If you're in a tight cash situation, you could always offer an incentive for a deposit such as free shipping or something extra on the order. It's sort of a give-and-take situation; you both get something you need. Solving a cash flow problem is well worth the discount or free shipping given to a customer.

Payment Discounts

Discounts for paying invoices and other bills early are used a lot in the business-to-business world. In the consumer world, payment is expected on completion of the service or delivery of the product, so there's no need to offer any discount. But in business, the invoice amounts are larger, and it's worth it to offer a discount to fast payers. Many times, the amount discounted is made up by the late payers who end up paying service charges. Discounts can speed up much-needed cash flow from monies due and reward your best customers. Don't hesitate to use them often, especially when you need to increase cash flow. Entice your customers to take advantage of the discount and highlight the words so they are easily seen. If they don't know about the discount, how can they act on it? If we really need the payment quickly, we will even call a day or two before the discount date and remind them.

Then there's always the question of whether to offer a percentage or flat amount discount. I always preferred the flat amount because it looks bigger at first glance. Imagine looking at an invoice for £6,000. Then you see that there's an offer for a two percent discount if paid within 10 days. Or it might say take £100 off if paid within 10 days. You can imagine in your mind what you can do with £100, but two percent doesn't create that mental image as easily. And two percent sounds so small, but is actually more than £100; it's £120. By stating an amount, you don't have to offer a set: even percentage amount, you just specify the discount in cash. I think you will see more people taking advantage of a discount that's specified in cash rather than a percentage.

You need to set terms to receive the discount, otherwise there's no reason to offer it. A lot of companies use the phrase *paid within 10 or 12 days*. This actually means that the customer just needs to post it by then, doesn't it? Once the cheque is written and put in the box, it's considered paid. But to me, *paid* means when I can cash the cheque or deposit it in our company account. Otherwise, it can get lost in the mail or mishandled and delivered late. It is really the payer's responsibility to get the payment in the hands of the receiver. That is why when we offer a discount, we specify, *received by X date*. This helps in two ways: we must receive it by a certain date, not just a number of days. This speeds up our monies due by several days when we offer discounts.

Get Invoices Out Quickly

When you need to speed up your cash flow and get paid early or on time, make sure your invoices aren't delayed. By *not delayed*, I mean the same day the product is shipped or the service is rendered. There is no reason to wait any longer than absolutely necessary. Set up a programme in your company to get all the information necessary to generate an invoice to the person doing it, immediately. And if the person who processes outgoing invoices is off or on another project, don't wait until tomorrow; have a backup person. Stress to everyone in your company that invoices must be processed and out the door as fast as possible. If additional charges to the order are realised after the invoice is sent, just generate a second invoice with those charges.

If you have a lot of smaller invoices (under £500 each) be sure they get mailed the same day they are printed. Use first class postage and make someone responsible for getting them in the post *before* the last collection time printed on the box. If there is no post box nearby with a late enough collection, the post office usually has a central posting box that's available until 6-7 p.m. When we have larger invoices (£500 or more), we send them special delivery. This way, we're reasonably sure they will arrive in two days at the latest. In many cases, if the invoice is large and we're offering a payment discount, we will fax a copy before we post it with a post-it note saying *your order shipped today*. This lets the customer know that their order is on the way, and alerts them to the discount available. You can also use email for this purpose by sending a copy of the invoice. Then you can stamp the invoice as *faxed* or *emailed* before you insert it into the envelope, so there will be no confusion when it arrives.

I think eventually, if not sooner, the practice of mailing invoices will become obsolete. Everything will be sent via email from computer to computer. The person who needs to approve the invoice will do it without printing it out and forward it to their accounting department. It will be automatically scheduled for payment and given a payment date. When that date arrives, the money to pay the invoice will be electronically transferred into the vendor's bank account. An email will be sent from the bank to the vendor's accounting department letting them know the amount they have available. There will be no delay to wait for a cheque to arrive or clear because it will be instantaneous. There will be no bounced cheques, either, because the computer will stop them from going out electronically if the money is not there.

When Your Customer Is Late With Payment

It's a fact of business that some of your customers will pay you early, some on time, and some late. There will also be times when large corporations will tell you the terms you must accept if you want their business. You need to decide right from the beginning if their business is worth it, and, if you can live with those terms. Make sure you are making enough profit on their orders to justify the longer terms.

When you print your invoices, be sure your terms are easily seen, not hidden. In fact, the terms of payment should also be on all your quotations and price requests. It seldom makes a difference to the buyer up front, but could make a difference to *you* later. About two days after the invoice due date, we fax a reminder to the customer, if it has not been paid. We will sometimes get a call saying they never received the original invoice (which they did because it never came back). We immediately fax another copy and call an hour later to make sure they received this one. We also ask how quickly they will process it and mail it. This tells them that you're not just going to let it slide for another week or so.

If the invoice is still not paid in another five days, you can fax a second reminder or call the accounts department. If they have voice mail on, leave a detailed message with the invoice number and the fact that it's currently overdue. Leave your name and phone number and request a return call. We like to also say that if we don't receive a call back, we will call again tomorrow, and then do it. Once they know you're going to continue calling, you're likely to get a response. Always be professional, and you should get the same treatment from them. The people paying the bills have a job to do just as you do, and it's easier when they are dealt with in a businesslike manner. If several calls to the accounts payable person don't produce any results, you need to try another approach. Try calling the person who placed the order and ask for their help in getting your invoice paid. Many times, they will ask the accounting person to give you a call back with the information you're looking for. If approached correctly, most people will be happy to help you. Being nasty or demanding with the person who orders can only jeopardise future orders.

If customers or their accounting department call you and say they would like to pay now, but are having some financial problems and need more time, the first thing you should do is ask for a partial payment *today*. Accept any amount they offer, but don't accept zero. Even a small partial payment will show they are sincere in getting your bill paid. Then you can set up a payment plan for the balance that they can live with. It's better to request a smaller weekly or biweekly payment rather than just one monthly. If they do end up closing their business, you will have at least some of the money owed to you. In most cases though, your customers will pay off the entire invoice throughout a longer term. You can then decide, based on how they handled the payments, whether to extend full or partial credit in the future. Just because they had trouble paying on time doesn't mean you should write them off forever. They may become a loyal customer if you helped them through a tough period. People tend to remember those who helped them through difficult times.

Make It Easy to Pay You

What does this mean? Of course it's easy to pay: Just give us the money. But how many different ways you will accept payment is really what we're talking about. Sure, most companies will accept cash, cheque or money orders. But if you also accept credit cards, you may open the door to more customers and faster payment. Credit card companies will deduct anywhere from one to three percent from the amount being paid before or after depositing it in your account. Your customers may like the fact that they can get miles or points by using their card for business purposes. Plus, they don't have to write a cheque, sign it, and post it to you. It's quick and convenient for them, and they have a record of their payment on their statement. Always closely guard any credit card information given to you, and file or destroy the card numbers. If it's not going to be used again soon, we put it through the shredder.

Another idea for assisting your customer in paying is to provide a self-addressed return envelope with the invoice. This can be without postage, or a business reply envelope for which you pay the postage, plus a small fee when received. Because this is not for advertising, I prefer the envelope without postage. It just makes customers' jobs a little easier, and you're assured of no mistakes when they address the envelope. In the past, I've used a pastel envelope, which is easy to find and stands out in the mail stack when you receive it. Don't we always open the envelopes with money in them first?

Finance Charges

When you're paid on an invoice past the normal due date, you may want to add finance or service charges. These charges can also offset any discounts you offer to early remitters. The amount you want to charge can be set up in your computer accounting program and printed on the customer's statement. The common amounts that most businesses charge are 1 percent, $1\frac{1}{2}$ percent, or $1\frac{3}{4}$ percent per month on any unpaid balance that's past the terms. For regular customers or those that are only a few days late, you can override or credit these charges. For others, let them pay it. Most customers who plan to do business with you in the future will pay the finance charge within about 30 days. Each month, your computer will add another finance charge to the balance of any amount that is still over the terms that you set up, so you can continue to pile up charges for customers who become real problems.

For finance charges to become legally valid, they must be specified, and the debtor must be alerted in advance. You can't just send customers a bill for charges that they didn't already know about. It's not valid or legitimate, and can't be enforced. The best way to state your finance charges is right on your invoice. And don't make the print so small or hidden that they never see it. We write a bold sentence stating that a finance charge of 1½ percent per month will be added to all amounts not paid within 30 days of the invoice date. They can't miss it, and it may help our bills get processed a few days earlier. That's really the purpose of a finance charge—*to get paid on time*. You don't say you're not going to use your credit cards anymore because they add a finance charge every month. Of course, you're not offering a revolving charge, but there is a fee to go past terms, and they should expect to pay it, so state your terms, finance clearly, and collect your money.

The Tough Ones

If you send out enough invoices, you'll have some extremely slow payers. In fact, you'll get the feeling that a few may never pay. I'm not going to say that it's just part of being in business because I don't believe that. You should be paid for 99 percent of all the invoices you send out. If you do the correct advance checking and request a deposit on first orders, there's no good reason in my mind why you shouldn't be paid in full. I didn't say there won't be some tough ones to collect from, but you need to have a policy and procedure in place for them. If it's a first-time customer, you learned a lesson about them, and this should be filed or noted on their account in your computer. Don't let another order get through entirely on open credit; make sure all employees know your procedures.

A procedure for collecting the older invoices (more than 60 days) is to stay in constant contact with the person responsible for paying them. If they always have voice mail on, leave a message each time you call and let them know when you will call again if you don't hear from them or receive a payment. When and if you reach them, request a partial payment on the spot with a credit card or a cheque number that will be sent *that day*. Keep asking when they can pay the balance or at least another partial payment. See if they will set up a schedule for partial payments and stick to it. Also, smaller payment amounts will have a better chance of clearing the bank. If they miss a scheduled payment, call them the next day to see what the problem is. If they can't make the full payment, try to get as much of it as you can. Just keep the money coming, even if it's small amounts.

When the payments stop or never start, you need to move to the next step. If they order regularly, you will have to stop shipping your products until they catch up on some of the past invoices. But if there is little else you can do yourself, you have to turn the monies due over to a collection agency or a lawyer. This will cost you anywhere from 25 to 50 percent of the amount owed and add even more time to collecting it. If you let it go much past 90 days, your chances of collecting anything get much slimmer. So when you feel you've exhausted all your abilities to collect it yourself, turn it over to the pros and hope for the best. I always hate to do this to a customer, but what other choice is there? You provided a product or service and didn't get paid. Do what's necessary as a last recourse, and don't even consider writing it off until you have exhausted every possible effort.

CHAPTER 16

Cash Reserve

Isn't it great when your business is doing well and cash flow is not a problem? This is what all your hard work and investments are supposed to yield, but don't sit back with your feet up on your desk just yet. It's great to get there, but it may be even harder to stay there. Business is similar to poker, in which you get hot streaks and then some not-so-hot streaks. You may have outstanding products and services that your target market can't live without, but your dominance probably won't last forever. Competitors and new people entering your market will be chipping away at your good fortune. So if your market share starts slipping in one area (and it probably will), you will need a reserve to finance your business while you're looking for that next great idea. You don't want cash flow problems interfering with your new idea process.

So the time to start building that reserve is when you are on the up. That is usually when there is some excess money available that's not committed to other expenses. That's when you need to use any funds you can to build a cash reserve, and cash reserve doesn't mean putting 50-pound notes in a shoebox or savings account. It means planning ahead for what you will need if sales are less than what they are at your peak time. Remember all the high-tech companies who thought their good fortune would never end in the late 1990s? Maybe 10 percent survived, and I bet you can't even think of the names of some of the others that are gone forever. They spent money and expanded like their wallets had no bottom. But when their markets tightened up and their stock prices went south, they went to the cupboard, which they found was bare. The cash reserve they needed to keep the company alive was not there. They didn't think they needed it because they had blinkers on. They could only see in one direction and didn't bother to look sideways or backward. Let's face it, even when you are having a good dream, you *will* wake up eventually. Reality will always be waiting for you.

I believe that if you want to stay in business for the long term, you need to establish some type of reserve for a rainy day. Don't keep your head above the clouds; come down and see that the weather can change. Be ready when it does and you can use your skills to work on your business instead of your cash flow. And as most of us know, chasing cash takes a lot of physical and mental energy. It can take over your daily routine and leave you more exhausted than running three miles! Establishing a cash reserve is like preventive medicine; it's what you do *before* you have a problem that can positively affect the outcome. Studying before a test will give you a better grade than not studying at all.

Separate Bank Accounts

I've always been a firm believer in not mixing apples and oranges; they each have a separate use. In all of my small businesses that had employees, I always had a separate account for payroll. It was either at the same bank as our general account, or at a completely different bank. Just before payday, I would transfer the amount of money needed for payroll, plus a little cushion, into the payroll account. When making the transfer deposit, I would also check the balance in there to be sure there were no surprises when wages were paid. This was also the account that paid income tax and national insurance.

If you operate more than one business or under different business names, separate accounts are a good idea. In this case, I always open an account at a different bank from the other accounts. If there is ever a problem with one account, you will always have a different bank and account as an alternative. Because it takes some paperwork and time to set up, the existing open account is ready to use. It may also make it easier to know which expenses were charged to what business. And you will be building a relationship with two banks instead of one.

164

Things that could adversely affect your bank account are usually done before you even know they are going to happen. If the bank calls in a loan or credit unexpectedly, it could take all the cash from your account and leave you with outstanding cheques that won't clear. You will find that you agreed to this and the bank has the right to do it. Remember all that small print in the contract that you didn't read? It's in there somewhere.

Another no-no is using your personal current account for business. Don't combine personal and business expenses together; keep separate accounts, even if at the same bank. I would recommend having your personal account at a different bank. And don't keep all accounts under your own name, even if you are an independent professional. For any account used for business, always use Inc., LLC, Esq., or just print *professional account* under your name. This way, there won't be any question about which account has paid business expenses. Have the bank send the monthly statement and any other correspondence directly to your business address or a PO box. (In the case of a home business, definitely use a PO box at a local post office.) Money can easily be transferred between accounts electronically. You can check your bank account on the bank website or by using their phone banking service. Electronic transfers are fast, so using several separate accounts is simple and easy.

Now you may think that several different accounts are going to cost you a lot more in bank service charges. This is not always so; you can speak to a business representative at the bank and ask for reduced or free services. If you explain how you are going to use your accounts and the amount of money you think will travel through them, you can often make a deal. A lot of small deposits will cost the bank more to process, so if you can group some together, there will be a saving there. Explain to the bank how you plan to grow, and that you will probably use some of its other services. Even if you don't follow up on the other services, once your deal is set, it won't change, unless you rock the boat.

Ready Cash and Credit

You could always put extra cash for a rainy day in a cigar box, safety deposit box, or under your mattress. These are all well and good, but the cash gets a little bulky, and you have to keep counting it. I'd rather be out playing golf than getting arthritis in my hands from all that counting. And two other disadvantages are *no interest* and *no insurance*. Your homeowner's policy might cover some of a loss (minus your deductible), but it's very hard to prove the total amount. And it may be too tempting for some of us when you see that expensive dress or fishing gear on sale. Cash is nice, but not really the most practical solution.

A better idea for stashing all that money you are saving for troubled times is somewhere you can get to quickly, and is both secure and can appreciate. I think the worst place, but still better than the mattress, is a regular savings account. You can open these at your bank in your company's name by completing the necessary paperwork. The interest is so low, you'll need a telescope to see it, but it is secure and readily available. Just be sure that they don't charge any extra service charges, which can cut deeper in the already low interest rate. Banks are a little like casinos—they don't offer you anything unless the odds and edge are in their favour. Streetwise businesspeople know that banks are a necessary evil, but you'll never get rich on bank deposits.

A little better alternative to a savings account is a money market fund. They still pay low interest and the money is easily available, but the rate can move up and down more often. I prefer a money market fund with a major broker instead of a bank. They usually charge no fees and can be insured by a policy that covers you to a million dollars or more. A money market fund can be a good choice if you put money in and take it out often. If using a broker or IFA for your account, make sure there's a branch nearby and you know their open hours. Money should be available by cheque within one or two hours, and some accounts may even work like a current account such that you can write your own cheque if you want a withdrawal. If you also buy and sell stocks, request that any money that's not invested is automatically put in your money market account.

If you have credit with a bank or home equity loan, pay these down when you have any free money available. This should be a no-brainer, but how many of you are actually doing it? Credit firms charge high enough interest that paying them down actually saves you more expenses. And remember, this money is not gone; you can borrow it back at any time. So why pay interest when you don't need it? The bank or lender also likes to see that you have paid extra money back, and that makes you look good if you need to increase it someday.

Another type of credit is the overdraft. This is usually easily available and the interest is not too high. But why pay even this interest if you can pay down some of the balance? Once you're below your limit, you may want to ask for a credit limit increase. That's when banks want to offer you money—when you don't need it. But if you get an increase when times are good, the extra money will be there if things change for the worse. Unfortunately, I've now heard that some banks have started to charge a yearly membership or maintenance fee for this type of account. If you can find one without it, choose that, but they all will probably follow the other bank's fees.

Another place to put cash that can be available again in about two to four days is a mutual fund in the company's name. I know they always tell you to invest for the long term, but that's their disclaimer. If you feel you can handle the risk of some fluctuation in share price, then put up to half of your reserve in a growth mutual fund. Your intention should be that you won't need to draw it out soon, but you can if necessary. There is no guarantee of course, but the market has always recovered in the past, and gone on to new heights. Unless you want to be a stock trader (which to me is a full-time job in itself), a mutual fund offers some security and liquidity.

Other Non-cash Reserves

When your resources are a bit above average, there are other ways of establishing reserve backups that aren't really cash, but will allow you to use them as an expense now and use later. These are items that you regularly need to pay for, but may be able to accrue in advance. Then when and if finances ever become tight, it's one less expense to worry about. It may not seem very important to devote money to these things in advance, but you will be happy you did if cash flow slows down. It's sort of like going to the dentist to get your teeth cleaned. You may not see its importance when you're doing it, but you will wish you had if problems arise later.

Here are some things that you can consider investing some of your excess cash in:

- Prepay insurance premiums and add any additional coverage you feel is now necessary. Check with your agent or company rep to see if you can receive any discount for paying a year in advance. By getting ahead on insurance payments, you can be assured that any unexpected events in the future will be covered financially.

- Stock up on stamps or fill your postage meter with some of your excess funds. This is a necessary expense that is used every day in good times and bad. They never expire and any large amount can be listed as an asset on your financial statement as prepaid postage. If you are planning for a future big mailing, you can also make a postage deposit at a reputable mail house.

- If you are able to pay your suppliers early, within 10 days or on delivery, you may be able to negotiate some payment discounts. Most can be convinced to give you 1 to 5 percent off your invoice for fast remittance. And if you help them speed up their cash flow, you are going to move way up on their favourite customer list. This will pay off when you need something special or a rush delivery.

- Start taking advantage of larger order quantity discounts. Stock up on your best-selling products before costs rise or delivery gets slow. As long as you have storage or warehouse space available, and the products won't become obsolete, this can actually increase profits if the prices on those products increase.

- Do some things for your employees that you can't do when times are slow. Have lunch delivered (pizza, chicken, Chinese), which is paid for by the company. Give out any overdue bonuses or gifts for a job well done. Most will remember this when times get tough, and work hard for the company. Keep your employees happy when you can afford to do it.

- Buy stuff you know you'll need soon or in the future, if it's on sale now. This is the time to take advantage of all those bargain offers you get in the mail. Have one of your staff scan and review all the sales literature you get to find products that you order regularly. Also look at your wish list and select a couple of items to get now.

- Is there any equipment maintenance that needs to be done now or in the near future? This means manufacturing machines as well as office equipment. Do it when you can easily pay for it, because if a breakdown occurs during tough times, it can be a real disaster. Review all warranties and user manuals, and get all the preventive service when it's most affordable for you.

- Now is the time to stock up on expensive office supplies such as copier and laser printer toner, pens, copy paper, and so on. As long as you know you will use them, fill up your storage cabinet.

- Do any research or product testing when you can more easily afford to pay for it. The secret to reversing a down-trend later may be a new product or service you find now. Do your investigation early, so you're ready to move quickly should the need for new ideas arise.

- Start your customer appreciation programme and give those valuable patrons things such as promotional items, loyalty cards, scratch cards, and other little bonus items. These will not always fit in your budget, but keeping your name in front of your customer is always important. If you were planning on giving your best clients a holiday gift, get it early and be done for the year.

- If you are planning to exhibit in or attend a trade show or convention within the next 12 months, pay for some of it now. Pay off stand space, furniture rental, and on-site costs well in advance. Buy those plane tickets and re-serve hotel rooms early, and you may get the best prices and the best availability.

- Buy any other future travel tickets up to a year in advance and you will usually get the best prices. If you are planning on visiting other cities, branch offices, or suppliers, this can be done and paid for. You won't have to consider cancelling or changing your agenda later if business slows down.

- If you use a lot of printed flyers, catalogues, or brochures, consider buying a year's supply in advance. You may be able to order a larger quantity and get better prices. Because you probably won't be in a rush for delivery, the printer can combine your order with others and provide a saving for both of you. Also, do any updating or create any new literature when the money is there to pay for it.

- Do your test mailings of direct mail pieces while you can easily pay for the cost and postage. You'll be ready with a new prospect list if business should change. This can be a good time to see if you can add a new segment to your target market base. You might start getting new customers that will head off that slump that may be coming.

Being prepared in advance is one of the streetwise survival techniques that work for everyone. So don't wait for it to start raining before you buy your umbrella—have several of them in the closet. Similar to the weather, the sun can be shining one minute and shortly thereafter a storm begins. And remember, it even rains in the desert once in a while, so don't think it won't happen to you and your company. This is one reason that you see a big corporation get into a slump and its stock drop 50 percent or more. The company is driving ahead with blinkers on, and didn't plan for any setbacks. Its people are not prepared and can't always react quickly, but if you're streetwise, prepared, and plan ahead, you can dodge those puddles and survive until the sun comes out again.

CHAPTER 17

Shoddy Bookkeeping

Keeping track of sales, expenses, payroll, cost of sales, and profits is a necessary part of every business. We all know this and try to keep good accounting records and reports, I'm sure. Sometimes it even becomes drudgery, and gets put off or temporarily pushed to the side. Even the streetwise entrepreneur will sometimes neglect "the books" in favour of a more rewarding task in their business. It's a lot more fun and challenging to work on marketing and promotions than to enter figures in a journal or computer. But those numbers you are entering into your bookkeeping system will tell you what you can spend on marketing and everything else. Numbers don't lie as long as you're using the correct numbers and all of them are entered.

Once you start to get behind on bookkeeping, it may be difficult to catch up quickly and accurately. If everything is not entered and accounted for when it occurs, you may forget or lose some of the figures later. I had a business once where one of my key people that approved factory invoices became lax and let them pile up in a drawer. When we started to get *overdue* notices on some of them and investigated, we found more than £10,000 worth of them were not entered into our accounts payable. So all of a sudden, we owed £10,000 more than we thought we did and most of it was due *now*! When something like that happens, bookkeeping moves from the back burner to the front very quickly. Telling someone that you had an accounting snafu just sounds like another excuse for not paying on time. It may be the truth, but it still doesn't sound good, and puts you in a vulnerable position.

Most small business owners don't have an accounting degree, but may have taken a basic course or two in high school or college. That's really all you need if you have a business accountant or bookkeeping service. You need to know what goes into what account and how to read and understand the results and reports. If you need a refresher course, you can probably take a short seminar or class at a further education college, business school, or even on the internet. It is important that a business owner understands the numbers even if someone else is doing them for you. There are times when your business seems to be doing well, but the numbers show that maybe it's not and vice versa. So find the time to review the reports regularly and investigate anything that looks unusual. Letting it go can just make an undesirable situation worse.

General Bookkeeping Fundamentals
Accounts Receivable

This is a number you want to see as big as possible as long as it's within your terms. All the items you sell and have to invoice are listed here until you collect payment. In a shop, this amount will be much smaller because of cash sales and no invoices being used. At least once a month, you should review an ageing report, which shows how old the invoices are. If you ever apply for a business loan, an ageing report will be required regularly for lender review. Usually, any open invoices that are older than 60 days will be discounted and not used for any collateral basis. You should have some type of collection procedure that kicks in when invoices due to you go past your stated terms. I always felt that you should never be embarrassed when trying to collect your money. You provided a product or service and deserve to be paid according to the terms that were part of the transaction.

Accounts Payable

This is a number you would like to see as small as possible because it's the money you owe. All the invoices you receive for any reason should first be approved to make sure they are correct and then be listed in this account. An ageing can be done to see which ones are the oldest or nearing overdue status. It also can help you plan ahead if you see something large that will be due soon or is due now. There will be times when you know you can't pay everything within the terms that are expected. For open invoices that fell behind, refer to Chapter 5 for some ideas. When your payables amount is more than your receivable amount, then you could be in for some rocky times, but not knowing is even worse, so read the reports.

Cash Flow

The money that travels in and out of your business can be both positive and negative. The more cash flow you have, the more flexibility you will have to pay your bills. If you're paying out more than you're collecting (negative), you need to work on either end or both. Without a constant flow of money, your business can become stagnant or even crippled. If you can't seem to get control of it, you'll need to take a time out and create a budget you can live with and be able to finance. Many lenders have been looking at a company's cash flow numbers as a basis for the ability to repay any loans.

Cost of Sales

These are the major things that make up the product or service you are selling, such as manufacturing, freight, or what you pay a supplier when you buy wholesale. You will either pay up front or be invoiced for them. You will want to keep these bills as current as possible, so there will not be any interruption in your product supply line. It's like a restaurant: if the food is not coming in the back door, it won't be going out to the customer tables in the front. What you sell your products for minus the cost of sale is what your gross product will be.

Expenses

These are all the things that are deducted from your gross profit and the cost of doing business. Some of these are fixed amounts (or about the same each month) such as rent, phone, electric, and so on. Whether fixed or not, they have to be paid if you want to keep operating. They may not be as critical as cost of sales items, but they will catch up with you eventually. If you don't keep a good record of what you owe and when it's due, you can be in a hole rather quickly. Some of these items can be trimmed back a little during slow times if they are not fixed.

Payroll

This could be your biggest expense along with all the employer added taxes. You should know what your payroll is weekly and monthly. If you pay people by the hour instead of on salary, you need to verify any time sheets you use, or have someone you trust check them. You must keep track of all deductions for taxes, insurance, and any investment plans. In some cases, you will need to provide a report to employees on the amount deducted for various items. And if reports and payments for taxes are late or incorrect, there could be penalties as shown in Chapter 23.

Staying Up to Date

You have several choices of how you want to do your bookkeeping, but you must have at least one workable way. Someone has to do it, and if it's not you, then you need to select another way. When selecting a person or service to handle your books, don't always look for the cheapest. Use a person or method that you feel the most comfortable with and you can afford. This usually means that the cost will probably be in between the lowest and highest. Reliability is another factor to consider; late reports and other information will do you more harm than good.

In-house bookkeeper

This is someone you hire either full time, part time, or once a week depending on your business volume and the amount of work needed. Be sure they have accounting or bookkeeping experience, preferably with past small businesses rather than large corporations. And they should be familiar with payroll taxes and the required reports that need to be paid and filed. If you can, check at least one reference and inquire about reliability and accuracy in their work. They should be able to work well with your accountant and understand all the terminology. Don't try to hire a good one and pay the lowest wage, be fair and even more so if possible. They will save you money in the long run, and provide valuable information you need to operate your business.

Computer software

Another in-house method is to use one of the popular accounting software packages on your own computer. You will need to learn how it works or hire someone who has used the specific software before. If you aren't going to do all the input and reports yourself, then you need to assign a reliable person on your staff to do it. And there must be at least one back-up person plus yourself that knows how to use it in case your key person is off, on holiday, or leaves the company. Your back-up person can even be a spouse if they have some bookkeeping background or take time to learn it. Most of the software packages available have different levels available, and you should choose the one that best fits the size of your company and gives you the reports you want. In most cases, you won't even use half of what it includes. But just like any other computer report, it's only as good as the data that goes in.

Accounting service

There are still several national and many local services where you send (or they pick-up) copies of all your cheques, sales reports, and cash transactions, and they do the rest for you. These types of companies were big in the 1980s and 1990s, but some have disappeared with the availability of in-house accounting software. If you don't have anyone to do it on your staff, this is a possible alternative. They should have all your tax reports done on time and remind you to file before the due date. You should also receive easy-to-read financial reports monthly (or quarterly if you're very small) including a balance sheet and income statement. The income statement should have the current period plus year-to-date information. Another nice report to receive is a cash flow statement, but you may have to ask for it. You don't want to get behind on paying the accounting service bill because if they interrupt your service, you'll be left in the dark. At least quarterly, you should have your accountant review your reports for any errors and to offer you financial suggestions. When looking for an accounting service, talk to at least two or more people and call a few of their clients. Don't just hire the lowest price, check everything out first.

Accountant

Let me start out by saying that every business needs a business accountant or CPA to oversee their financial reports, offer advice, and assist in any tax problems. Unless your small business is a hobby and you have very few sales, get a good accountant. Many of these wise men or women will offer a bookkeeping service as well, but it could be a little more expensive than others. If you can afford it, do it, but don't expect your accountant to personally handle your day-to-day general questions; they get paid too much for that level of work. Your accountant will assign an account manager who will report to them. That's the one you call when you have those everyday questions. They should also be more available and get back to you quicker with any answers they don't know on the spot. Depending on the size of your business, you should actually meet with your accountant quarterly, semi-annually, or at the very least, once a year. You are paying them for their advice, and you should get it face to face.

Other Considerations

Shoddy or incomplete bookkeeping can cause problems for any company. If your bank account is not reconciled with the bank statement monthly, or at the very least, quarterly, it can result in bounced cheques. If it happens only once in a while, well that's business. But if it happens often, that's a dangerous problem that must be solved quickly. Most people will deposit a cheque twice, and if it goes through, you may be okay. But you need to find out why it didn't go through the first time. If you are still using the float (sending cheques before deposits are made) you must know that new computer technology is getting the cheque back to your bank more quickly now and the money needs to be there.

Another reason your bank account may be off or too low is that a deposit or merchant charge did not get credited. That is why I check every bank statement to make sure all deposits are credited before I look at anything else. This can put your account overdrawn faster than anything, and you need to find out what happened *fast*. If you don't have a local rep for your merchant account (credit card processing) then you should have a free phone number to resolve any questions and problems. I keep the number and my merchant number taped to the side or bottom of the machine for quick access. I have found out a few times that just because you were given an authorisation number doesn't mean that the money will always be in your account overnight. There are times when a charge might be put on hold for an investigation for a variety of reasons. They are supposed to notify you, the merchant, right away, but like anything else, it may not happen when it should. If this has happened much too often, I'd consider changing your merchant service company. After all, if you're spending money that you think is in your account and it's really not, there will be big problems.

Also, check your bank statement to see if any cheques you have written are not cashed after they are 90 days old. Where are these cheques? Did they get lost or misplaced? Did the person you gave the cheque to forget to cash it? Is it sitting in a drawer or file somewhere? I would suggest that you or one of your staff contact the recipient and inquire about it. If for some reason they didn't receive it at all, you can cancel or put stop payment on it and reissue another one. Letting it drag out any longer just makes more bookkeeping work, and you are never sure when, if ever, it will hit your account. If it's a larger cheque, you want to know where the money is, and that you're not overdue on some old bill.

Part of your bookkeeping job is being aware of how customers are paying you if your business sends out invoices. Many owners get lax in this area because they have no time or are afraid of offending their customers. Well, when you provide a product or service and have explained the price and terms in advance, you have the right to get out there and collect your money. This is why you are in business in the first place. You can start by faxing or mailing an overdue reminder and then someone should call about a week later. If you, the owner, don't want to do it, then designate someone on your staff to do it. Keeping good records of accounts receivable is always important, and the business owner should review a weekly aged report. Don't let these overdue monies get too old; this is the money you need to pay your own bills, and if you're not even sure who owes it, well, need I say more?

You should also have some type of system in place to check *every* incoming bill to your business. You need to make sure you are being charged at the price you agreed upon, the quantity is correct, and any deposit you made in advance has been applied. If you are paying by cheque or credit card, a date, amount paid, and how you get paid should be recorded on your copy and filed or kept in a computer record. You also want to be sure that you don't make any duplicate payments, which may be difficult to get back later. Some of your vendors and others will automatically send you a refund, but others might put you through hell trying to prove it.

If you think your bookkeeping system and records are out of line, take the time to straighten it out before it really hurts your business. Most entrepreneurs dread this part of their job, but should realise that it's very important. If necessary, set aside one rainy weekend, go over the way you do things, and make any necessary changes. Add any new procedures that you need, and have a meeting with your staff or key person to get the new process going. Staying current and accurate with your accounting will give you a true picture of how your business is really doing. Without accurate accounting, how do you know if you are even making a profit?

CHAPTER 18
Pricing Problems

Deciding on a price for your products and services can be a bigger challenge than most small business owners realise. It would be easy if we could say that we want to make £100,000 this year, so let's set our prices accordingly. All you need is to sell X number of those products and you will have the income you want. It's so simple, what's the problem? And why can't we all have 2.5 children: one boy, one girl? You don't need me to tell you that some decisions are more difficult than others, and you keep second-guessing them as you go along. There are a lot of factors that go into setting your prices, and those factors will change constantly. So, you need to also change your thinking as needed when pricing your products and services; what was a good price last month may not be today.

Your prices can be the lead or secondary factor in your marketing. As a small business person, I feel they should be behind the scenes and not your main selling point. If you get into a price war with the big boys, you can forget about winning—they just won't let you. Or they will out-advertise you so that your target market won't even notice your low prices. Price wars and almost giving away your products is for companies who have little else to offer. How can you be the lowest price and provide the best value at the same time? Something has to be sacrificed when prices are severely low.

You will notice that the same products and services sell at different prices in different areas of the country, or even your county and local area. Just look at the crazy petrol prices. Even the same franchise brand will have different prices at different locations. I think the type of clientele will dictate the price level for most locations. The big hamburger chain will price a little higher at the motorway services than in a normal outlet. When you're talking about lunch, a traveller will pay a little more for a good product with quick service. You obviously need to know your market and play the game accordingly to be successful in pricing. In my opinion, pricing your products correctly is not an art, it's a science based on many facts and conditions. Then again, maybe there's a little art involved, if you get to know the attitude of your customer base. And as new information is obtained, adjustments along the way will be necessary.

Competitors Are Everywhere

Incorrect pricing in a crowded market can send your customers flocking to competitors' doors. This doesn't necessarily mean not being low enough; it means being the right price for the right value. People expect to pay for what they get, and if the price is too high or too low, they start wondering what's wrong. You expect a hamburger to be under £3 and a designer suit to be more than £150. If the suit was £25, and if you were a trendy businessperson, would you really want it? When you go to the movies and see outrageous prices on popcorn, sweets, and drinks, you think twice or three times before buying anything. The queue wouldn't be so long anymore, and you would have a difficult time selling anything at those prices at a store outside the cinema. Competitors would eat you up (pun intended) in no time, and the public would probably laugh at you. But in a cinema or an airport, there are no competitors, so if customers want it, they pay.

But competitors won't always dictate your pricing guidelines if you provide good reasons for higher value. Higher value can justify higher prices if the customer *wants* the higher value and recognises it. If the customer doesn't care about a greater value or doesn't believe that it's there, they may baulk at a higher price. You must *prove* to them that its worth more, *not just tell them*. Remember, it's the benefits to them that count, not the product features. Why would a customer want to pay more for a drill that not only makes 1/4-inch holes, but 1/8-, 3/16-, 3/4-, and 1/2-inch holes if they will never need more than 1/4-inch holes. All the selling in the world is not going to convince them to pay more for that drill unless it's just to keep up with the Joneses. It's like selling ice cubes to an Eskimo; it may be possible, but it won't make you rich.

Your competitors are constantly trying to figure out ways to steal your customers, and pricing is one of the weapons. If they have no tool in their box other than beating your price, I think that makes it easier for you to fight back. And I don't mean fighting back with even lower prices—that only gets everyone lower profits. Fight back with *value* and show why your product or service is the better deal at a higher price. Use weapons such as better quality, guarantee, selection, benefits, and reliability to prove your point. These all must be true, or your customer base will just ignore your claims in the future. And once your reputation is tarnished, you might as well change your name and move to another town. Don't claim, advertise, or stress things that you can't provide, or the tables will turn on you quickly.

If you can't find enough qualities that make your products a higher value, then you need to get busy and make some changes if you want to compete. If your competitors are showing that *they* are a better value, then your sales and profits will start slipping, and may turn into a downhill slide. They want to beat you in your target market just as badly as you want to beat them. If you open the door, they are coming through, and it will be difficult to get them out. Smart competitors will only make you better at keeping your prices and value in line. You are also their competitor, and they are watching you, even if you don't see them.

When you raise or lower your prices, will your competitors follow you? You see this all the time in airline fares. If one airline reduces prices or has a sale, it seems everyone that serves the same route matches them within five minutes. And what will you do if *they* increase or decrease prices? Will you follow, or stand firm and wait it out? If you reduce prices to match a competitor, will your profits suffer? Is it worth it? Because if you're just matching competitors' prices, you probably won't increase the number of sales. So, without increasing the number of sales and selling at a lower price, you're making less money (a.k.a. profits). Don't feel too bad though; your competitors also have to answer these questions. Changing prices to increase sales seldom comes out a winner.

What the Market Will Pay

You have your own target market: the prime customers and prospects who will purchase your product or service. If you have a tight vertical market, there may be fewer competing products available, so you can possibly price a little higher. Experience in your market will tell you how high you can actually go without hearing grumbling from your customers. For specialised products or those with patents, it's a little easier to get less negative feedback about your prices. Competitors may have similar products, but they won't be exactly the same. So if your benefits outweigh theirs, price may be less important to completing the sale. Just don't get too carried away and make your prices so high that you force buyers to look at other products with fewer benefits. You're driving them to other products from your rivals when the sale was yours.

What the market will pay means that customers are comfortable with the value they received for the price they paid. And as long as they are comfortable, why should they even bother to look around? They might find a lower price, but is the same value there? It's your job to make sure it's not. If you're trying to sell at the best prices you can get, then you have to prove to your customers that it's worth it. "What you see is what you get" is not good enough anymore unless you're selling at bargain basement prices. People won't buy at a clearance sale unless the prices are really low. But if you want the highest price that your customers will feel comfortable with, you need to provide some uniqueness backed by superior customer service.

Remember that pricing at what the market will pay is exactly what it says. It doesn't mean setting prices at what *you* want to charge; that will provide negative results. Look at the expensive luxury cars; they are priced higher than the average car, but not out of reach for most professional people. Some people may have to stretch their budget a little to afford them, but if they want the car, they do it. You can be assured that the luxury car makers would like to tack on another £5,000 or £10,000 to the price, but they don't because it would be out of reach for many buyers. They want to sell as many cars as possible to as many people as possible at the highest affordable price as possible. You don't want to lose many customers because your price is more than they value your products.

Why You Need to Raise Prices

There comes a time in every business when you need to increase your prices to stay profitable and keep your head above water. If this never happened, we could still buy bread for 25p a loaf and a business suit for £20. It's a fact of business life, and everyone knows it. You and your competitors know that this will happen from time to time, and have learned to expect it. But when the time comes, it's still not easy to do, without getting some unwanted feedback. Some business owners are afraid to raise prices because they think all their valued customers will run away to other suppliers or stores. This is rarely the case if you have done the rest of your job correctly. If you have provided great value along with outstanding customer service, there's little need to worry. You're not going to lose many customers because of a reasonable price increase. And the few that may exit your domain will probably be back when they see that the grass is not always greener....

When it's time to raise prices, *it's time to raise prices*. Have the courage to do what's necessary to keep your business successful and profitable. Don't hide behind a lower price that is less than the value you're offering. Did you ever see a heart surgeon charge low prices just to get more patients? If he's a great surgeon and can save lives, price doesn't even come into the picture. Most of us think that lawyers charge too much, but it's soon forgotten when they help you win your case. And when their costs go up, so do their client prices; everyone pays it because of the value that's there. Here are a few reasons why you must consider raising your prices:

- *Increased product cost*—It doesn't matter whether you purchase your product ready to sell or you manufacture it yourself—costs will increase. And when costs increase, they eat into your profits if you don't raise your selling prices. If raw materials go up, it affects everyone in your industry.
- *Payroll and benefits*—To ensure good productivity and superior customer service, you will need to compensate your employees well. They will want periodic salary increases and the cost of their benefits will continue to rise. You need to look at these cost increases at least once a year and adjust your selling prices to accommodate them. Good employees create value for your customers.
- *Rent and utilities*—Your landlord is probably a nice person, but when it comes to annual rent increases, landlords are all business. Even if you own the building, your real

estate taxes will increase regularly. Plus, your electric, gas, water, refuse collection, and everything else connected with your physical location will want more of your money. The extra amounts have to come from somewhere.

- *Marketing and advertising*—These costs will go up along with everything else and must be compensated for. But don't just cut back in these areas to make up for any increases. That's a bigger mistake than not raising your prices. Marketing is the engine that pulls the rest of your business, and you don't want growth to come to a standstill. Cutting back here could cause you to have a slow period, and then more money is needed.

- *Competitors raising prices*—It gets to the point at which even your competitors can't wait for you to increase your prices. They may feel it's time to do it for any number of reasons. This is your opportunity to silently follow without too much said in your target market. You'll want to increase by a similar, but not exact, amount. How will you know how much your competitors have raised prices? By shopping with them, being on their mailing list, and visiting their website. If you don't know that they have increased their prices until 60 days afterwards, you're not doing your job.

- *Other higher expenses*—Your shop or office may need a facelift or repairs, and this will enhance your customer's value. You might be adding people to your staff to serve buyers faster and with increased services. Delivery and packaging costs may have increased. You might be adding new displays or literature to better present your products. Unless you have a box of money buried in the basement, these new things must be paid for from somewhere. A reasonable increase in prices is a better choice than taking out a new loan. Your customers will also see something that has come from your increased revenues.

Pricing Tactics

Where do you want to price your products and services—high, low, or in the middle of competing products? There's no right or wrong answer here, but you should be consistent. Whatever level you choose, stay there, and don't jump around. You'll confuse your customers if you keep changing from low to high to middle and so on. And buyers don't like to buy at a place that confuses them. Think your tactics out thoroughly before you make your move. Once your decision is made, stick with it for at least six months to a year before considering changing. This will give you enough time to see it in action and determine if it's working. For short-term changes in price, use a special sale to reduce prices and clear out products.

If you decide that you want to offer low prices, then most of your competitors will always be chasing you. You'll have to be alert and watch all sides to see who's going to attack your prices next. Low prices are only worth all the aggravation if you can significantly increase the number of sales and still make a profit. And increasing the number of sales will take more customer service people (who have to be paid) to process those orders. There will also need to be more order follow-up and solving of problems with returns. There will be more invoices to send or cash sales to keep track of. And with increased invoices, there may be additional delinquent accounts to chase after. So, you'll have more products to move around, more paperwork, and more computer input to process and less profit per order. You need to decide if the increased sales you must get from lower prices will pay for these expenses, plus still show a profit. Do you know what amount of sales you need to show a profit? If you can't answer yes, you'd better find out, because once your market labels you as the low price company, that perception will be difficult to change.

Another consideration for offering low prices is your sources of supply. What will you do if you lose a major supplier of either raw material or finished products? Things such as fire, weather, mergers, or just getting behind on your factory invoices can halt your incoming supply quickly. Because you need this incoming supply to keep operating, you'll need an alternative supplier or two. But what if the alternative supplier won't sell to you at the good prices you were getting? Can you continue to sell to customers at your low prices and make less, if any, profit? And if you quickly raise your prices, will you lose some of those bargain hunters? When first buying from a new supplier, you may need to establish credit, which takes a while. Or the supplier may request full or partial payment on the first few orders. Where is this money going to come from? Low prices are nice for your customers, but you open a can of worms when there are problems. And selling at low prices makes it look like as though you have nothing else to offer. Do you?

Selling at higher or middle prices where you can show that you have added some value to your sale is safer for a smaller business. Most of your competitors will pay less attention to you because you're not trying to beat their prices. The only time you may consider reduced prices is during a special sale or clearance. And because it's only temporary, your business rivals may not attack. Fluctuations in supply won't be as serious if you have a little room in your prices. You'll be known in your market as the company with value, quality, and outstanding service instead of trying to beat everyone's price. Your customers will be more loyal and less swayed by your competitor's price-cutting. You may have a few less regular customers, but your profit level will be more stable.

By not trying to be the lowest price, you can direct your marketing to get the potential customer in the store, to your website, or on the phone, and your value-added service can take over. If your marketing and presentation are done correctly, buyers won't expect the lowest price—just a fair price for the value and service they are receiving. This gives you the time and money to make your product or service at the level they expect. You won't need to spend the majority of your time trying to figure out how to be the lowest price. Let your competitors fight it out among themselves to be the lowest price. You will have your own loyal group of customers who will not only like your price, but how you sell it. You will also attract others from the low price crowd who are tired of sacrificing value and service for just price. If you treat them well and don't disappoint them, you will build your business with new loyal customers, not only price shoppers. And price shoppers will change to the next low-price seller with very little loyalty to anyone. It's hard to build a solid long-lasting business relationship with this type of clientele.

Another pricing tactic that can be used by a small business is to offer a sort of rebate to first-time customers. The rebate is not in the form of a cash refund, but as a credit or coupon to be used only by them on a future order. It can be 5 or 10 percent of the amount of their current purchase. It also needs to be used on a minimum order amount that you set. This is used so they are not getting products completely free or as much as 50 percent off. You will also want to set an expiry date of three months, six months, or a year. You should also keep some record of all of these you give out. They are similar to gift cards or certificates with conditions. Using this method can help ensure that your new customers will come back a second time. After the second purchase, you can hope that the third, fourth, and so on, will be by habit.

One more idea for attracting customers is to accept your competitor's coupons if you are selling the same or similar products. This is usually a pleasant surprise for customers and can make them feel at home quickly in your business. If you are going to do this, you must advertise it and make sure that potential customers know *before* coming to your business. The purpose is to get them in contact with your business rather than going elsewhere. Once they're in contact with you, they don't need a coupon or discount, you've already got them. Use this idea only to bring them in instead of offering it in-store or on the phone. The objective is to make that first contact.

If your business is involved in doing quotations for potential customers, here's another idea I've used for business customers. On our quote we put in bold letters that we are offering a certain flat or percentage discount if they place the order by a certain date. We don't use *a* number of days; we use an exact date, about seven to 10 days after the quote date. This can help you get orders in two ways: one, you get the order faster and have more time to deliver on time or early. Second, it gives the buyer less time to shop around and get a better price. It also makes the customers feel they received a little something extra for no real additional effort. Most people like to receive something for nothing.

There are many other pricing ideas you can come up with and not use the obvious low-price idea that everyone else is using. Tax your imagination and find new ideas that will interest your target market. Pricing can be a problem or an opportunity depending on how you play it. But remember, if trying to be the low price, you're really no better than most of your competitors. And if you're not better, why should anyone new buy from you?

CHAPTER 19

Losing a Big Account

How good do you feel when you first acquire a new big account or customer? Let's not deny it, we all feel pretty good and love to pat ourselves on the back. Big accounts are so difficult to get that you enjoy the moment while you can. It compares to winning the semi-final of the FA Cup; you celebrate briefly then go back to work and try to win the next big one.

Once you've jumped over the first hurdle and captured a new big account, your work is far from over. The real challenge is keeping them satisfied so they will remain customers for as long as possible. During your courtship, you should have found out some key points that made the customer decide on you for their supplier or source. The customer/buyer expects you to provide what you promised without having to remind you. This goes for all the people in your company that they come in contact with. There is no excuse why Jennifer in customer service didn't know and Bob in shipping didn't either. It's your job as owner or manager to inform *everyone* of any special arrangements that have been made for this big customer. And informing them is not enough; you must check and recheck that things are being done just as promised.

This means that if you agreed to 40-day terms, they don't get an overdue notice on the 31st day. Or if you said that you would call when a large shipment was about to be delivered, you do it promptly. And if you promise to ship in two weeks, they shouldn't be calling you after three weeks to find out where it is. It's always easier to do what you agreed to, on time, than try to explain why you didn't. And all it usually takes is a little concern and follow up along the way. Most reliable businesspeople will back up what they say they will do, even if it's not written down.

It usually takes a lot of time and money to acquire a new customer, especially a big one. All this effort reduces your profit on the first order or purchase, and you make less or break even. This is done because you feel that you make it all up on future or subsequent orders for as long as you can get them. There are many reasons you can't control that will make you lose the big account, but why let *any* reason that you *can* control do it. It's really foolish to take a chance losing a profitable account because of poor follow up along the way. Did you notice I mentioned follow up several times already? Well, it's not enough. *Follow up* will save accounts and create solid loyalty in others. Go to a novelty store and have them make 3-inch badge that say *I always follow up*, and have your employees wear them. You can also make signs and hang them in your office or store to remind everyone that it's part of their job.

When you have a big order and the customer calls to find the status of it, you should have an answer ready. And the answer shouldn't be "I'll check and call you back." Some current information on their big order should be handy and available if you're doing your follow up correctly. You don't get large orders every day, and if you want to get a second chance at it, you'd better pay close attention to the first one. In fact, you can and should be faxing or emailing them progress reports *before* they ask. You want to give the customer the confidence that they placed the order with the right company, and it shows that you value their order which is always appreciated.

Confidence plays a big part in keeping a big account happy. Without it, there may be reluctance in placing another or future orders. Whether you can see it or not, you're probably on probation during your first order, and that will determine whether you get a second one. Many large companies are a little reluctant to give a big order to a small business in the first place, so you need to earn their trust. Without trust and confidence, would you keep working with a supplier?

Why You May Lose a Big Account

Error on an Order

There's nothing as bad as having a product delivered or a service done and it's not what the customer expected. Errors and misunderstandings happen more often then they should, and sometimes it's a fine line of how to handle it. Even if it's your fault, save the customer. And how long will it take to make it right? What was once a two week delivery is now four weeks because it has to be done again. And what if the error is the customer's fault for not checking proofs, samples, or specs along the way? If the value of the order is large and the customer is at fault, you need to decide if they are worth doing it again at your expense. How long and how many future orders will you need to make up for this lost revenue? And will the customer actually reorder after this problem? It's a tough call, and you need to make a decision.

New Order Person/Buyer

Very few people remain in the same position forever. Buyers, similar to everyone else, move up or move on. If you haven't become acquainted with others in the department you sell to, the new buyer may have some other vendor in mind to supply your products or services. This happens all the time in big accounts, so be prepared. Don't just assume a new person will automatically just keep doing things the old way; they may want to make some changes. Get to know them as soon as possible, and show your value to their company. You may need to sell the account all over again, but don't ignore the chance.

Moving Out of Your Market

If you only supply to a local or regional market, and deliver products or provide a service to a large client, you are vulnerable to relocation. If your customer moves out of your market area or closes a plant or office, how will you service them? Is there a way to open a branch location to service where they move to? But keep in mind that if you lose their business again, how will you pay expenses that you may be tied into. Just because a corporation has been in one location for more than 50 years doesn't mean they won't leave. It can and does happen.

191

Merger or Buyout

There's something that you not only can't control, but you may not even be aware of until the last minute. Big companies keep all these plans and negotiations behind closed doors, especially if they are listed on the stock market. The surviving or dominant company may not be your current customer, and the responsibilities for purchasing your type of products or services may change. The department and/or people you currently work with may be transferred or even eliminated. Purchasing may be combined, and you may have to earn the business all over again or lose it completely. There's not much you can do in this case because the decisions will come from top management.

Conflict With Customer Employee

A long- or short-term relationship with your customer's staff can sometimes become rocky. It's best to avoid confrontations that can only cause bad feelings in future dealings. Even if you feel your position is right, that doesn't make it practical to insist that it be accepted. And if you go over someone's head to a higher person or a supervisor, that doesn't mean you're going to come out ahead. A supervisor or manager will most likely side with an employee over an outside vendor. You could lose their business either now, or in the future.

Specifications Change

You may be providing a product or service for some time and all of a sudden, your big customer wants to change it. If you can supply the change, great, but what if you can't? Do your big orders that you count on come to an end? The answer is probably yes and there's not much you can do about it. Maybe they will not need any of your products at all and stop buying. If you're selling big orders of cassette tapes it won't last forever.

New Competitor

Someone is always trying to come up with a better mousetrap and steal everyone's big customers. Yours are no exception, and your new competitor's reps will be talking to them. You probably won't even know its happening unless you're close enough to your buyer that they will tell you. Many large companies feel an obligation to look at new products and new vendors to assure themselves they are getting the best products at the best prices. Be aware of what's going on in your specific industry, so new innovations won't be a shock when they sneak in your customer's door. You should also be working regularly on improving your own products that will compete with these new competitors. Playing catch up may make you look desperate.

Slow Payment

Losing a big account can also be a result of your own doing. If you find that the time it takes to get paid is long and getting even longer all the time, you may need to reconsider their business. Obviously, you will make all the efforts you can to resolve this situation but sometimes you just can't seem to. If the extended payment time leaves you in a *no profit* or a *break even* position, it's not worth it. You have your own bills to pay, and the money for them needs to be there when you want to access it. Cutting off or firing a big account will almost bring tears to your eyes, but when it has to be done, do it. You can't put your entire business in jeopardy because of one customer, no matter how big they are. Your first responsibility is to your company and your employees.

Take Their Business for Granted

Many times, a long-term business relationship will get you to be too relaxed and actually *expect* their business. But I've been a part of these situations, and they can change when you least expect it. Assuming that you're *always* going to get the order is a mistake you don't want to make. Any company, especially a large one, can change direction before you have a chance to respond. Be sure you value every order, and let your representative at the company know it. Without you knowing it, they may be getting pressure from above and be required to check other sources. Even if you have a contract for a specific time or quantity, big accounts can usually find a way to break it citing quality or late delivery. Treat their business like a weather forecast, which can change at any time.

They Go Out of Business

Unfortunately if this happens, you can lose two things: the customer, and the amount they still owe you for past orders. In some cases, you can see this coming, but other times, you're caught off guard. Some indications may be that you notice that they are paying invoices a little slower than in the past. And you should be paying attention to how your big accounts pay you or insist that your accounting person keep you informed. But sometimes, you can be surprised when you least expect it. In either case, never let one account put your company in jeopardy by extending more credit than you can safely cover from other accounts, and check their website periodically. The sooner you know about an impending problem, the sooner you can plan to minimise its negative effects.

Your Customer Service Dept Can't Handle Them

There may be a situation where the customer service rep or reps in your company just can't seem to understand and accommodate the needs of a big account. There are communication problems on a regular basis, and you are constantly called in to mediate. After a while, your customer may become frustrated and take their business elsewhere. When you see this starting to happen, you have a few choices: handle the account yourself, replace your customer service rep, or just let it happen. Sometimes, the situation may even correct itself without intervention. Either way, it's a tough call, and you might be scratching your head trying to come up with the correct solution that keeps everyone happy. Rash decisions usually don't work, so take the time to analyse the problem before you make your move.

They are Too Much Trouble

As much as it might bring tears to your eyes, a big account can sometimes cause more trouble than they're worth. They can disrupt your company by putting too much pressure on your employees and suppliers. The never-ending badgering, requests, demands, and unreasonable changes can put you in a position of wondering if you're really making a profit on this account. And if you're not or just breaking even, why bother? Their orders may look good in your sales totals, but at what other expense? When that other expense gets to the point that it's affecting other customers or the morale in your company, you may need to stop it. You can ask to have a conference with a person of authority to see if there is a way to resolve it before making a final decision. Don't insist on ultimatums, but explain the situation, and see if a mutually agreed upon solution can be arranged. If it can't, I'd say phase them out gracefully.

Argument With Your Rep

This should really have no place in business, but it does happen on occasion. Your sales rep or assigned customer service person just can't seem to get along with the key person at your big customer account. The sooner you become aware of this, the sooner you can change it. Figure out a way to put another person in this position or even handle it yourself for a while. If you ignore this situation, it could eventually turn nasty and seriously jeopardise the entire business relationship. You will always be getting a bad rap for your company, and they may be on the lookout for a new vendor. A quick call to see how things are going from time-to-time is a good idea.

After It Happens

When the unfortunate happens and the account is gone, don't just write them off forever. In many cases, you can get this customer back with some effort and perseverance. This pertains mostly to accounts/customers lost for reasons you could have controlled. Stay in contact with them to see how things are going with their new vendor. Are they really satisfied with the quality, delivery, service, and personnel that they are now using? They should know in a relatively short time whether the new vendor meets their expectations. Remember, they left you for something better, and if they're not getting it, the door may be reopening for your company. Make sure you're available when and if this happens, so they won't have to come looking for you. If you're doing your homework, then you should know about the same time they do. If you're not ready to jump in immediately, they may be inclined or forced to seek out a third party.

Once you have a new chance to reacquire your big account, make it easy for them. If their new vendor didn't meet their expectations, don't start saying "I told you so." Gracefully move in and assume the main vendor position in a very businesslike manner. Keep personal feelings out of it and provide everything they missed and expect. Have a short meeting with the people on your staff that will handle their account and provide outstanding service and availability. If you have learned a lesson from the entire situation, remember it and use it in other accounts. Don't let it happen again or there may never be another chance to get them back.

CHAPTER 20
Cash Flow Shortfalls

Lessons learned from real-life experiences are usually not forgotten easily. I've certainly been taught quite a few over the years. These are experiences you don't learn in school, but unlike a textbook education, these actual experiences are long remembered. The small business owner rarely lets the same preventable situation ever happen again. It can be your gut feeling that sometimes solves a problem in real life. Just like a poker game, sometimes you have to play the player rather than the cards. It's been said that cash flow is the lifeblood of any business, because if it stops or slows down, so does everything else. Just like the human body, if the blood stops flowing, nothing else works. And if there is not a quick fix for the situation, surviving may not be possible. For bills, employees, and everything else that needs to be paid, money must continue coming in the front door. When and if that door closes, the balance sheet becomes empty quickly. And if you want your business to grow and prosper, you can never let that happen. Cash must flow through your business continually to ensure a good relationship with your employees and suppliers.

When cash is low or is coming in slower than what you need to pay your obligations, it soon moves up to a top priority. Things that need to be paid now are put in an order of urgency, and there is not much else that can prey on a business owner's mind more than needing money. I've been in this situation many times, and it really ruins your overall game plan. It's hard to concentrate on marketing, personnel, and new ideas when you are having cash flow shortfalls. When a short-fall in cash is happening, it becomes more important than profits. While profits are key to the overall health of your business in the intermediate and long term, they can be put on the back burner for short-term emergencies. What you need first is money, so you can buy and sell those profitable products again. As I said earlier, without it, everything can come to a standstill.

The worst thing you can do is to ignore a cash flow decrease, because it will only get you in deeper trouble. You must be able to recognise it early and be prepared to deal with it immediately. Any delay will only accelerate the problem. It's like a snowball rolling down a hill; it keeps getting bigger and bigger until it's too large to manage. A cash flow problem is not the end of your business; it's just one of those potholes on the road to success. It just seems to be a major interference in your day-to-day operation. Nonetheless, it is a part of doing business, and you need to know some streetwise ways of handling it. By having solutions in place in advance, you will be able to manage this situation more effectively. The road to recovery may be smooth or bumpy, but you must be on it to reach your goals.

Know What You Need

The first step in managing a healthy cash flow is projecting how much money you will need for expenses, supplies, payroll, marketing, investment, and a cash reserve. If these change at different times of the year, you can make projections quarterly or month to month. If you will need to hire additional employees because of seasonal changes or growth, that also needs to be factored in. Also, if there is any equipment that will need to be replaced or upgraded, add that to your cash requirements. Don't forget future raises for employees and the constant increase in the cost of benefits. You can get many of these numbers from the income or profit and loss statement that your accountant gives you.

There will also be needs for cash because of unpredictable events (Chapter 21), and many of those may be immediate. You can't let your business stop operating for more than a very short time, or some of your customers may look elsewhere. Customers and clients will feel sorry for you and your problems, but their businesses and lives must go on; they may not able to wait very long for you to recover. In most cases, you will need money to get you back on your business feet again.

Now if you have a cash reserve (Chapter 16) or credit available, that can be used right away. But if not, you may need to use money from your cash flow or incoming monies. This of course takes money away from paying suppliers and/or expenses.

One method I use when I'm in a restaurant or a bar on a trip is to make a list of expenses. I'll grab a piece of paper or a cocktail napkin and start writing down numbers. Without any financial reports, I'll see if I really know what my expenses are. I make a list of rent, payroll, postage, printing, insurance, and so on. Then I figure out what amount of sales I will need monthly to pay these on time. If I add another employee or two, how will that affect my expenses and needed additional sales? Then when I get back to the office, I'll check my list with the latest income statement to see how they compare. I always seem to forget things on my list, which shows me why I need to keep cash coming in at an acceptable rate. This is a good exercise because it shows how much you really know (or don't know) about the money you are spending.

The ideal situation would be to have all our bills paid within terms, our credit cards and overdrafts down to zero, and a nice cash reserve fund. But unless your name is Bill Gates, it's not going to happen. Let's not kid ourselves—owning and operating a business is hard mental work, and cash flow problems are the ones that give us the most headaches. But knowing what range of cash flow you need (minimum to maximum) is a good starting point, and will allow you to react faster when it's necessary.

When Cash Flow Falls Short

Because we don't live in Utopia, the perfect situation pertaining to cash flow never stays perfect for too long. At one time or another, you will need to supplement it in one of several ways. This has to be done to keep expenses and suppliers current, and to meet your payroll requirements. If you have a cash reserve (Chapter 16) or overdraft, great, you know where you can get money fast. If it's a short-term problem, you can use high-limit, low-interest credit cards. You can also try to raise money quickly (Chapter 22), but some of us will occasionally reach our borrowing limits. If you're using a secured loan and housing values have gone up, you may be able to get a quick limit increase there.

There are a few other ideas that may produce a boost in your cash flow other than borrowing. Use these as needed, and save some of them for future shortfalls that may show up:

- Sell off obsolete or slow-moving inventory quickly. Make the reduced price be an offer customers can't refuse. Just do it fast and require advance or COD payment, because you need the money now. Contact previous buyers, and if you feel the inventory will appeal to a wider audience, you may consider listing it on eBay or another internet auction site. Just keep your price low enough to move it fast.

- Don't pay your bills too early. Check the terms or the due dates and mail them to arrive just in time; keep that money in your bank account as long as possible. If you are spending £2,000 a day on bills and can delay your payments just five days, it's like getting a free £10,000 loan or added cash flow.

- If you need to purchase any expensive equipment for your office or factory, consider leasing rather than buying. This will save cash now and let you pay over a longer term. Always try to obtain a lease that lets you pay off the balance at any time without any prepayment penalty. When cash flow picks up again, you can increase payments or pay it off.

- Use a bank lock box for incoming payment deposits. The bank will immediately put the cheque into your account and fax or email the information to you.

- Use a bank that makes your deposited funds available immediately or within 24 hours of when they are deposited. You don't want to wait five days for the cheque to clear before you can use the money. If you're a new business, it may take six months to a year before the bank feels comfortable enough to do this. If the bank says that it never does this, it's time to look for another bank.

- Deposit large cheques with a cashier in the bank rather than using an automatic deposit machine. You will have a receipt from a real person, and you know that the money will be in your account. Any discrepancy from using an automatic machine should be solved, but may take a couple of days to do so. You want to know that the money is in your account now.

- Know the cut-off time that your bank has for same-day deposits. Always make your deposit before that time, so it's in your account today rather than tomorrow.

- Don't have all your expenses come due at the same time of the month. You can always call the company and ask them to change the due date. If you request to change it to an earlier date in the month, they should consider it.

- Ask your accountant for ideas to manage your cash flow. After all, you are paying for his or her services knowledge. Accountants work with a lot of other businesses and can use ideas they see elsewhere to assist you. Don't be afraid to ask; that's what they're there for.

- Don't order supplies or raw materials earlier than you absolutely need them, because when they ship to you, an invoice will be generated for them. And when it's issued, the due date time starts ticking off. Many large companies use a "just in time" inventory system that provides them with deliveries right before they need them. Talk to your suppliers and see what you can set up.

- If you have bills and invoices due for payment and you know that there will not be enough money available to pay all of them, try this: instead of just hiding them in a bottom drawer where you can't see them, send a partial payment and a note. In your own handwriting, write a memo saying how to apply the enclosed cheque, and that the balance will follow soon. This should buy you a week or so while you find ways to increase your cash flow. Just ignoring the bill completely will start more aggressive collection procedures and interfere with your daily routine.

- Collect your own outstanding invoices as quickly as possible to get that money into your cash flow. Some ideas for doing this are in Chapters 15 and 22. Check your monies due often to see who is overdue and almost due. Then act on it right away to keep cash moving in.

- Ask your representative at your bank to immediately re-deposit any returned cheques a second time rather than just sending them back to you. If it is returned again, ask them to call you right away, so you can act on it. At that point, the amount will probably be deducted from your account balance. Get on the phone immediately and re-quest a new valid cheque sent overnight or a credit card payment.

More Thoughts on Cash Flow

Always reconcile your monthly bank statement with your current account figures within a week or two of when you receive it. If your accountant does this for you, ask him or her to email or fax the results as soon as possible. The bank rarely makes a mistake, but you might, so you need to correct it as soon as possible. It's always nice if an error is in your favour, such as a missed deposit, but life isn't always that fair. You may have forgotten to deduct a cheque, credit card fees, automatic payments, or bank charges. You don't want to be spending money you don't really have available and take the chance that one of your cheques is returned.

If your bank offers overdraft protection (most now do), by all means, sign up for it. If you ever do run into a situation in which there are more cheques outstanding than there is money in your account, this will keep them from being returned. If the overdraft protection is big enough, you can also use it for quick short-term loans. Just remember to keep enough of it unused and ready to cover any overdrafts that may occur. Your monthly bank statement should also show you the daily balances in your account. This will tell you if you were ever close to an overdraft.

Most banks now have online banking that you need to register for using your home or office computer. This is a great way to keep track of all your transactions and see how fast cheques are coming back. You can also transfer money between accounts and pay some of your regular bills without sending cheques. Just remember that the money may come out of your account faster, and thus reduce your cash flow. So if you are going to do this, wait until the last day before the due date to make the payment. Every morning when I get to the office, I check our bank account for the current balance and to see which cheques came back since yesterday. This way I have no surprises later in the day.

If you have reached your borrowing limit, you can try to call your lenders to renegotiate a new agreement. Ask if you can add even a little to your credit limit, or ask if they would consider reducing your interest rate by a half or even a quarter percent. When you do this, there will be paperwork to sign again, but that may be enough to delay or skip your next payment. The amount not paid will be left in your cash flow. Also, I have made a deal with our landlord to let me skip a month's rent by adding a month or two to the end of the lease. This can be done easily by using an addendum rather than creating a whole new lease. Think of other ideas to delay payments or skip one to leave money in your account.

Even if you have enough money in your cash flow, try using credit cards for travel and office expenses. You will get a 20- to 25-day grace period during which no interest will be applied. Pay them off completely before the grace period is up, and in time, they will probably increase your credit limit. This is better than paying cash up front because you never know for sure when the next cash flow crunch will happen. It's like a free 20-day loan, which is hard to find anywhere else.

When and if your cash flow slows down, your fixed bills and expenses don't. So you need to have a lot of tools in your toolbox to try to fix it. Not every solution will be available and ready to use every time you have a shortfall, so keep all of them mentally handy. After these shortfall situations happen a few times, you will know which of these streetwise ideas work best for you and which don't. As I said earlier, when cash flow becomes a problem, it can take much of your time and effort to solve. But the sooner you can resolve it, the sooner you will be back on the road to growth and success.

CHAPTER 21

The Unpredictable

There's an old adage that says, "The unpredictable is, well, unpredictable", and of course, it's true. Things will happen in your personal and business life that you never knew or thought were coming. You can't stop them; you can only endure them and recover from them. Maybe it can be compared to falling in love—sometimes it happens quickly and sometimes throughout a longer period of time. Being prepared, or at least aware that things can and will occur, is the best defence or position in order to quickly recover. When you get an unexpected big order or new customer, that's the best kind of unpredictable situation. But unfortunately, most of the unpredictable occurrences you'll experience are going to be harmful to your business. Because there's almost nothing you can do to stop them, coping and recovering are the key to staying in business. And staying in business is what this chapter is all about.

You may think that fires, floods and natural disasters will always happen to someone else, but they do happen everywhere. The media tends to broadcast only the big ones with the most damage; sometimes you don't hear all about those small misfortunes. But if your business is in the middle of it, it's a big one for you. In most cases, people who aren't affected by bad unpredictable events are not going to worry very much about your business. It doesn't affect their lives, so why should they worry? You might get a "that's a shame", but not much more. To them, your problems are just a news story. You and your employees are the ones who will really care about what has happened and what you're going to do about it. Your employees will be looking to you, the owner of a small business, for all the answers.

And after an unpredictable disaster strikes, you're not going to get too much outside help without pursuing it. Banks and local agencies are not going to be standing at your door (if you still have one) offering you money and help. Help and assistance may be available, but you will have to go after it, and sometimes fight for it. Friends and relatives will feel bad for you, but can they help? Many times, people would rather throw money at a problem than spend any quality time solving it. But when the problem is yours, take what you can get and move on. If you don't expect too much help from friends, you won't be so disappointed when you don't get it. If you own a business, the problems are yours, and you can't expect others to care as much as you do.

The key to recovering quickly from unexpected disasters is to have a plan in place. But how many of us really do this? Because it's unpredictable, we don't think it's going to happen, until it does, and then it's too late to go back and make a plan. But whether you have a plan or not, you should have some written or mental preparation. Gather key employees together and have an informal meeting to encourage ideas and suggestions. Your best employees will be the ones with the most interest in a quick recovery. The meeting can take place anywhere and should be held as soon as everyone has settled down emotionally. If some people can't participate or don't want to be involved, go on without them.

Don't immediately discount any ideas that come up; write them down. Remember, the people in your recovery meeting are almost as eager as you are to get your business back to normal. Three minds are better than one and six are better than three. It may even be a good idea to let in as many of your employees as are interested, even if they don't participate. You'll need to assess each suggestion that comes up and see if it can be used or enhanced by the group. If you decide to use some ideas right away, most of the people who will put them into play will already be there. Anything that helps your business along the road to recovery is worth considering, so listen to everyone.

You'll need to compare and combine new ideas and suggestions with any previous plan you may have had. To get the most help from your employees, assure them that you will try to recover as soon as possible, and that their jobs are secure. If you were in their position, wouldn't you want to know that you can still provide for your family? You didn't ask for this major problem, and neither did your employees. But now that it's occurred, it must be dealt with, and quickly. Your being there is what your employees want and expect to see, so take charge and start the ideas to recovery going.

The next thing to worry about is your customers or clients. They will probably hear of your misfortune and wonder if they can still do business with you. Because you don't want to lose even one, they must be assured quickly that your business will be ready to serve them. If you have a company voice-mail system, record a message that answers the phone when you can't, and tells callers your plans. If you don't have a recovery plan yet, ask them to call back in a day or two when you have changed the message. You can also have calls forwarded to another number that you can answer, or leave a number in your message that callers can refer to. As soon as you can, alert all your customers of your situation via email, fax, or snail mail, and tell them what you're going to do about it. The sooner they hear from you, the less worried they will be about your continuing existence.

If you are a shop hit by an unpredictable event that closes your doors temporarily, you need to react. Try to get a sign made quickly that explains your situation and when you will be ready to reopen. Are there products or services that you can still provide while your store is closed? If so, let customers know how they can buy them. Can you keep one or more employees outside or near your location to meet customers and explain what is going on? If they talk to you or actual employees, they may not go searching for another place to spend their money if you will reopen soon. The more information you can provide, the more confidence customers will have in your recovery.

If you don't think it can happen to you, think again. In my years of owning and operating different small businesses, I can tell you firsthand that it can (and will). And, it can happen more than once in the life of a business. And so you ask what could possibly happen to my company? What are the odds of anything happening? Without using any official statistics, I can estimate that your chances of experiencing a business interruption event are about 40 to 50 percent every 10 years. In some cases, it could be much higher depending on your location and type of business. But really, no one can accurately predict what and when something will occur; that's why they are called *unpredictable.*

Let's look at some of these unpredictable events that can hold back your business or bring it to a temporary standstill. Maybe they all can't happen where you are located, but some can, so be alert and don't completely disregard them.

- *Weather*—Tornadoes, hurricanes, lightning, and heavy snow can last from one day to more than a week sometimes. Assess the damage and try to estimate the recovery time.

- *National disasters*—Even minor earthquakes can bring much structural damage to the affected area. Again, assess the damage and try to estimate the recovery time.

- *Floods*—These may occur with little warning, so get out while you can and salvage anything that's movable in the advance time you're given. But don't risk your life or that of an employee waiting too long to get out.

- *Man-made disasters*—Terrorist attacks such as September 11 can bring not just the entire business to a halt, but the entire country as well. Wars can take many military consumers away from you and reduce your customer base.

- *Fires*—Prevention is the real key here, so don't take it lightly. But if a fire happens, be quick and get insurance adjusters moving to a workable settlement. You'll probably have to rebuild or move.

- *The economy*—Fluctuations occur every few years, and that's normal business. But when the stock market really crashes, it's everyone's concern. People tighten their belts and your business can suffer big drops in revenue.

- *Accidents*—Chemical spills, train derailments, plane crashes, and other events that cause evacuations can be a problem. If you can't get into your business, you can't operate normally.

- *Crime scene*—If your location is the site of a crime, this can tie you up for hours or even days. The police have the authority to seal off any area in which they need to conduct an investigation. In high-profile crimes, this can be longer than you expect.

- *Employee injury*—Minor accidents and injuries may be a part of working, but sometimes a major one can happen. If it's serious enough, some of your employees may not be able to continue working for the rest of the day.
- *Power failures*—If your electric or phone service goes out, all your computers and internet connections go with it, cutting off your communication with customers and prospects. Depending on the severity of the problem, it can take hours or days to correct completely.
- *Key employee leaves*—When a person you rely on for years decides to move on, it can leave a huge void that will take a while to fill. Try to arrange in advance for employees to give at least a month's notice and give some bonus for not walking out.
- *Your death*—This is one that you can't help work out and should have a plan for. Things happen that we can't control, and there is no reason why your business should not go on. Your hard-working and loyal employees still need to provide for their families and should be able to keep your company prospering.

There are probably others that you can think of, which should tell you that *unpredictable* things can and will happen. It's what you do about them when they do that really matters.

The No-Brainer Precautions

Many years ago when I was starting out in business, it was a luxury to have a computer. Buying one was not the first thing on your list when planning a new enterprise. But today, you can't really exist without some type of computer system and the internet. They are as common and necessary as your phone system. Most businesses akin to yours will store many of their records on the computer because of its convenience and quick reference. So what would happen if one day it was all gone? Could you exist? Probably, but how long would it take to get back to normal—if ever? How much would a serious computer crash or disaster that wiped out all your records cost you? Can you even put a number on it?

209

The smart and sensible solution to a long, agonising comeback is to back up all files regularly and keep it off site. Update it often and take it home, or if your office is at home, have someone who is at least five miles away store it for you, such as an employee or relative whom you can trust to be there if the need arises. Be sure to keep it current and date the disk or CD with the date it was compiled. I would keep the last two dates in case there is something wrong with the most current one. You don't want to think you have a back-up file to rescue you only to find out that it was not done correctly. It's still better to back up two sets of records than to start over completely.

Another no-brainer is to have insurance. Most small business owners will be required to have accident and liability coverage, because if you are renting or leasing, the landlord will want proof of it. But don't forget to also insure your contents, which include furniture, computers, office machines, and all files and records. To keep the premium reasonable, select a higher deductible you can live with. You may even want to put an amount close to the deductible in a separate account that you won't touch. That way, it's there and immediately available should the unexpected occur. Plus, it's earning interest. Be sure to use an insurance company that specialises in all commercial coverage, or a good independent agent.

Another optional, but extremely helpful coverage, is business interruption insurance. You can choose policies that kick in after seven days up to about 60 days. Obviously, the sooner the coverage starts, the more expensive it will be. This type of insurance covers lost sales and profits up to a limit. You will probably have to show proof of past sales so that computer back up will come in handy again. If you can't operate your business or the unpredictable event won't allow you to function 100 percent, this type of cover will help pay the fixed bills. Each policy is different, but you may want to see if there is any provision to pay your employees some of their lost income if you are closed. Weigh the cost against the benefits and see if this coverage is for you. And always compare several companies before signing up; benefits and costs can vary widely.

Other Considerations

While your business is partially or completely shut down due to an unexpected event, keeping in contact with customers is essential. Your competitors will hear of your situation and be ready to pounce on your customers. Business is business, and any advantage is fair game. Don't leave customers in the dark and unsure of your ability to serve them. If they hear from you and get updates of your recovery progress, most will wait for you. Can you find a way to provide products or services to them through any other source? Even if your cost is higher, the fact that you are saving a customer is worth it. Look to future business— that's where the long-term profits will be. Keeping customers and assuring them of continued quality products and services should be a top priority. Once you're on the road to recovery, plan some type of promotion to give sales and profits a new jump-start. You want everyone in your target market to know you are back at full capacity.

If you have a retail location, a grand reopening may be just the thing to create interest and let everyone know you're open. Banners, signs, and ads can spread the word in your target area and bring needed customer traffic. Calls, letters, faxes, and emails to the media could bring some reopening coverage at no cost to you. Tying in some type of a sale or special offer will also bring a little excitement and entice people to come. Offering some entertainment and/or refreshments will bring in people that a normal sale wouldn't. You will want to do things that get people talking about your reopening. Word of mouth can often be more effective than any paid sources. You could also have a pre-opening sale for past customers on your mailing list. Send them a special invitation with a pass to attend before the general public.

If you are a business-to-business, non-retail type of company, you still need to create some interest in your comeback. You could offer anything from free shipping or a 10 percent discount, to rolling back prices to the previous year's levels. Do some advanced mailing, faxes, and emails to your customer list to let them know early. Remember that your competitors may have been in contact with them and you don't want to lose even one order or reorder. Once you lose an order to a competitor, it may be difficult to get that customer back. Your old customers will have been treated like royalty by your rivals. Of course, this is your competitors' job; just don't make it easy for them. If you're smart, you'd be doing the same thing if the tables were turned. New customers have to come from somewhere.

If you are an internet or home business, the damage to processing your customers' orders could be minimal. You could try to find another temporary source to fulfil your orders. You still need to notify all customers of any delays that are not part of your regular service. When someone expects delivery of something they ordered and it's not there on time, each day that it is late really drags on. Offer some compensation or a discount on future purchases to offset the inconvenience. Let them know that this is not your regular service and shouldn't happen again the next time they need you.

And when an unpredictable event happens to your business, it's really your problem, not your customers'. Don't go on and on about how bad things are and how much money you're losing. They may offer some words of consolation, but that's all they want to be involved with. The more you complain about the dilemma, the less confident they will be in your ability to serve their future needs. Come across with the assurance that you have the situation under control and everything will be back to normal shortly. Whining and complaining may just drive them into your competitor's open arms. Because you can't stop the unpredictable from happening, just start on the road to quick recovery. Most businesses can and will survive if you just don't panic and proceed in a businesslike manner.

CHAPTER 22

Raising Capital Quickly

There comes a time in the life of most businesses when you need money and you need it now! It can be a result of many things, but whatever it is, you need to raise capital fast. Maybe the need crept up on you slowly, and you didn't pay attention, but now it's a top priority. You may have creditors and suppliers calling to get paid, and this can really disrupt your day. Plus, your rent and utility bills are due. Why is it that when money is the tightest, these bills become due faster? Thirty days seems like 10 days, and paying one of them is always on your mind. Everywhere you turn someone has a hand out and wants to be paid.

I've been in this situation many times, and it never becomes easier to deal with. In fact, the solution you used last time may not work next time, or may not be available. So, knowing all of your options and weighing each one against the current problem gives you the best choices and solutions. Of course, knowing in advance that a tight cash situation is coming gives you more time to select the best way out. But how many of us choose to ignore a coming problem and assume that it will go away or solve itself? I can tell you from my personal experience that these financial thunderstorms *never* go away and seldom, if ever, solve themselves. They grow and grow and spurt off tornadoes that affect all parts of your business. Eventually, the situation that you put on the back burner is a raging fire on the front burner, which is threatening to burn your house down.

Part of running a business is dealing with these unpleasant situations and picking the best way out. The first time it happens, new business owners may show serious concern bordering on panic. But once you have all the options in front of you, a way out can usually be found. I've heard it said that at least 20 percent of an entrepreneur's time is spent figuring out how to raise money. Most of the founders of big corporations today went through these cash shortages many times during their growth. Nobody starts a business with a billion pounds in the bank; at least not 99.9 percent of us. So whether you want to remain small or take a shot at the big league, a constant supply of new money is sure to be a part of your ongoing plan. And the more choices you have to select from, the better the chance you have for a positive outcome.

Internal Choices

By being able to make the decision yourself, as the business owner, you won't get turned down by anyone else. These solutions to raising capital can be done quickly and be put into action today. They are just ways you rearrange the way you do business, and in some cases, they won't even be noticed. In fact, it is wise to have an advance file of how you would implement them, so you are ready to take action quickly if the need arises. Because when the need *does* arise, your mind will be clogged with thoughts of cash outflow and less room for cash inflow. Here are some things you can do internally to increase cash on a limited basis:

- *Offer payment discounts*—I have done this in our plastic card company from time to time when cash gets a little tight. We offer between $1\frac{1}{2}$ to 2 percent, and specify it on the invoice as a set amount, not just a percentage. We also highlight it and give an exact date when we must receive payment for the discount to be valid. If we really need the money, we'll call the larger ones a day or two before the cut-off date and remind them about the discount. About 35 to 40 percent of those customers actually pay faster to get the discount.

- *Speed up collections*—Don't let invoices or any type of payments due go past the date agreed upon. On the due date, according to the terms, we fax a copy of the invoice or payment agreement with the word *reminder* stamped on it. A second reminder is faxed or sent about three days later. And after eight to 10 days of non-payment, a friendly phone call is made to check on it. The longer you let it go, the longer some people will delay. And make sure they have your current address or where to send payment.

- *Change your terms*—If your business normally works by invoice (and most business-to-business transactions do), terms of payment are usually specified. The standard is about 30 days from the date of invoice, but it's not always the rule. Because you are the seller, you can dictate any terms you want. But don't go too extreme to the point that it would hurt your chances of getting business. Reducing normal terms to 25, 20, or even 15 days can speed up cash flow. If you are billing £3,000 a day and reduce your terms by just five days, that's £15,000 extra in your cash flow. Be sure that you make it well known on all invoices and literature, so there is no question about when an invoice is due. Some regular customers may give you a little argument about it, and you need to make a separate decision regarding whether to let them take a little longer.

- *Ask for a deposit*—This can be a standard procedure for all your orders or just used when cash flow is slow. In a retail situation, a deposit on any special order is usually a must. This protects you against the customer cancelling after the order has been started or disappearing when it's time to collect. We have asked for a 50 percent deposit on all first orders or from a customer who has not ordered for more than two years. To reduce paperwork on smaller orders, we require a 100 percent deposit on first orders, from people who don't have a permanent business address and phone, or a new start-up.

- *Stretch your payables*—As we discussed in Chapter five, some of your creditors are a little lax in their collections. These are the ones you can delay payment to for a few days longer than the others. But don't jeopardise your source of supply by not paying them at all. Sometimes even splitting the invoice into two partial payments will be acceptable to some creditors. If you normally have £2,000 worth of bills due each day and you delay half of them eight days, that's £8,000 more you have available.

- *Ship or deliver COD*—On new orders and those for which you have little or no competition, ask for cash on delivery (COD) or advance payment. If they wish to use a credit card, they can do so right before it ships, or keep it on file with you for any regular orders. This way, there will be no delays or collection charges when it arrives. Use this money to pay off old bills, and to keep products and services flowing from your suppliers. To entice some customers to pay in advance, you might offer a small discount or reduced shipping charge.

- *Raise prices carefully*—Increasing prices has always been a touchy subject for sellers and buyers. But higher prices will bring in more of that needed capital, so you should consider it. Select items or services that are unique or that you can provide a better value on. Hot commodity products should be left alone or be increased by only a small amount. You don't have to increase prices by the same percentage on every item. Vary the increase according to your ability to convince your customer that it's necessary. Raising prices is always better than reducing quality or service. It's always better to make a one-time increase than small amounts every month.

- *Sell add-ons or bundles*—Promote or push more things that go with a main product being purchased. When buying a computer, people will have an open mind on adding some software, cables, scanners, screen cleaner, or printers. Don't let that business walk out your door and go to a competitor. Many of these add-on products can also command a higher mark-up and generate more cash. Bundling groups of accessory items together can save the customer some searching and provide you with a larger order. Keep these bundled products or kits near the main product, so they can be found easily. Also advise your sales personnel to mention these to each customer, because many may not remember that they need them.

- *Carry products "sale or return"*—If a supplier is trying to talk you into carrying a new product, you may be able to get it "sale or return", which means you don't pay for it until after you sell it. There is no inventory cost and no accounts payable. Just provide selling space, and add to your catalogue or direct mail literature. This can also be done with bargain items and a big stock-up for a coming sale. Ask, fax, or email all your suppliers and see what their answer is. If you get 20 no's and three yes's, you're still ahead of the game. These items can make your shop or warehouse look fully stocked at a minimum cost.

- *Sell items on eBay and Amazon*—Do you have any products in stock that appeal to a mass audience? If there is a potential mark-up to be made on them, consider selling online. This will not only help you move products, but it will also bring some inexpensive advertising for your company. You may be able to pick up additional sales or repeat orders through email or direct mail after the sale. There are some auctions or online sites that specialise in specific product areas where your target customer may be looking. There are several books available for sale or in the library about how to sell on these sites. Read a couple and see if it can work for you.

- *Rent out space*—Do you have an unused space in your shop that you're not using to its full potential? Can you condense or combine some areas to make space available? Offer this space for rent to other people who are after the same target market you are, but are not competitors. The rent you receive will bring in needed cash and also generate a new customer flow. A written agreement is always a good way to avoid any misunderstandings. You should have final approval of any new products they might want to add to their stand. This can also work for seasonal sellers that don't want year-round selling space. You can also rent/lease any available warehouse or storage space you are not currently using.

- *Investment funds*—If you have started to put money away for investment or retirement, you may be forced to draw on it in an emergency. If there are no other choices immediately available, this is your money and you can use it. When things pick up, you will be able to replace it and more. Just remember that if you make a withdrawal from certain types of account, there may be a penalty. You need to decide if the situation and need for cash is important enough to pay the penalty. Make sure that the money you use will actually solve the problem at hand and not jut put it off.

- *Sell assets*—Is there any equipment, furniture, computers, vehicles, or other office equipment that you don't need or can do without? You could try to sell it to a used equipment dealer or list it on eBay, Amazon, or another auction site. Are there any soon-to-be obsolete products that you can greatly reduce the price on and get out the door? Try contacting previous buyers of these products and offer them a deal they can't refuse. Also, look to sell some of your personal assets at home. Would you consider selling personal items that you've lost interest in? If you can raise some money on these privately owned items, you may be able to reduce the amount you pay yourself for a short time and leave more in the business account.

External Choices

Family

This idea can be good or bad depending on your relationship with family members. There is probably always someone in your family who has the money to help you and your business, but do you want to ask them? It's usually a little awkward, but if you're going to pay someone interest, why not let it benefit a relative? You might even present it as an opportunity and offer a small percentage of the business without liability until the debt is paid back. Similar to any other loan or agreement, be sure to put it in writing and have both people sign it. Don't give away too much of the business now without an escape clause to get it back.

Friends

There can be a deep chasm between friendship and business. If you don't want to fall in, be careful how you structure any loan or deal with friends you want to keep. Don't let friends overextend their finances to help you, because what if something goes wrong and you can't repay them? Always have a written contract that spells out the risks and benefits for all parties. You may have friends with excess capital to invest, but you must convince them your need is a smart choice. Some will just help because you are a good friend, but don't betray them by putting their money in a high-risk situation.

Angels

Do you know someone who is more of an acquaintance than a friend but has adequate capital available for your current needs? These are personal investors (sometimes high-risk investors) who are looking for a good return for their speculation. They don't walk around with name tags on their chests, but they're out there. You can probably be introduced through business associates, your banker, friends, or even at the chamber of commerce meetings. Most of them will assess you and your business before making any commitment to invest. Once they decide to go ahead, they will probably back off and not interfere with the running of your business. Doctors, dentists, lawyers, and sports figures are a good source for angels. These are great sources of quick cash, but remember, they are looking for a high-percentage return.

Overdraft

This can be a great source of capital because you only pay interest when you need the money. You can borrow and pay back over and over again without any additional approval. You can use money at will and pay it off when you have it available. They can be set up at your bank. All the paperwork to qualify is done at the beginning, and as long as you follow the terms, you won't have to do it again except for some updates later. The smart way to do this is to set up the overdraft *before* you get into a cash shortage, so the money is available immediately. These are usually the best sources of quick cash because you control the purse strings.

219

Credit Cards

Here's another quick way to get cash, but maybe at a higher interest rate. If you've been paying on time, your credit limit has probably been raised several times. This makes more available credit when you need it most. You can always call and request an increase, which is usually answered in one to five days. But if you are going to use credit cards, it's better to pay a bill or supplier with the card instead of taking a cash advance. A cash advance commands a higher interest rate, and the limit available is often less than your credit card limit. Ask those you owe money to if they will accept your credit card as payment, but ask them *not* to keep it on file. You may even earn *points* or *miles* you can redeem later for trips or gifts. This is not as good as credit, but very handy when you're in a bind. Just be sure to make the minimum payment or more when it's due.

Bank Loans

Unlike an overdraft, a straight loan will give you a lump sum loan all at one time. Bank loans require a lot of paperwork, questions, and about three weeks before you get a positive or negative response. For working capital, an overdraft is better, but a straight loan (at a decent interest rate) is probably ideal for a big purchase or expenditure. You may also be required to keep your current and savings accounts at the bank making the loan. Banks like to have a close relationship with borrowers.

Invoice Financing

This can be done through a bank that will pay or loan you anywhere from 60 to 80 percent up front on invoices, and a little more after they are collected on time. But a more common way is through a factoring company, which does essentially the same thing. You turn over receivable invoices to the factor and they pay you right away, but not the full percentage. When the customer pays in full directly to the factor, they give you the balance minus their fee or cut. If it extends beyond 90 or 120 days, you must pay back the factor any advanced money and take the receivable back. You can find factoring companies in the phone book or on the internet. Check references before you use any of them.

Venture Capital/Private Placement

If you're looking for a larger amount of money for your business, say £100,000 or more, there are groups of investors that may be interested. These groups and sources will loan or invest money in your business with the hopes that you will strike it big and they will get an above average return. They will usually ask for some equity as security, and will want to see some sort of business plan. They are more interested in future potential rather than past performance. They will assess the situation, and if they are interested, make a deal. It can take anywhere from two weeks to two months for a deal to get done, so make sure you have the time and can wait. The thought of giving up equity will bother some owners, and it may not be the right avenue for them.

If you are interested in pursuing the private placement or venture capital route, there are two directories I have found in the reference department of the library. They list sources of groups or people who have money to invest and how to approach them. You can also check each one to see if you have the type of business that they are familiar with. Keep in mind that they don't just hand out this money to anyone, you have to prove that you are worthy of receiving it. Check with your reference librarian to locate these directories:

> VCR Directory—lists hundreds of venture capital firms in the UK. This free-to-use service features extensive information about each investor.

When preparing for a bank loan, private placement, or venture capital investment, pay a lot of attention to the material you submit. Financial statements that are soiled, contain typos, or are missing information will start you off on the wrong foot or even get a quick "no". Other areas that can cause a denial of new capital are having no business plan, low cash flow, excessive debt, and a management with little or no experience. Before you even approach one of these professional organisations, sit down with a good accountant and plan your strategy. It's always harder to go back later and create that desirable first impression all over again.

Is a Home Equity Loan Right for You?

For all of us who didn't win the lottery or have a rich uncle pass away and leave us money to start a business or finance a current one, we have to look elsewhere. Start-up, emergency, or working capital is always difficult to find because banks and other sources only want to give it to you when you don't need it. But if we want to stay in business and succeed, it has to come from somewhere, because without it, we're only flirting with danger when the ups, downs, and necessary expenses become due. I've seen so many small businesses have problems—sometimes severe—because they were undercapitalised. If you're *always* worried about money, it's hard to spend time building your business, so you need a ready source that's there for those spur-of-the-moment situations that come up.

Because I've never had a pile of cash available for the many businesses I've started, other sources had to be found. When I was younger, similar to everyone else, I thought the only way was to get a business bank loan. So I pledged everything, including our house and my next-born child, and got the loan. Not only was the bank triple-secured, but the interest rate was high—so high that when the market got very competitive, it was hard to make a percentage profit that was much higher than the loan interest. I decided then and there to seek out better sources than the iron-fisted bank. I was tired of feeling subservient to a bank loan officer every time I needed money. I wanted to have a little more control of my destiny.

So that brings us to the source of choice, the home equity loan. I've tried them all, and by far this is the best if you must borrow. But before you actually apply for this type of loan, be sure you understand how it works and what the risks are. We all get offers in the post, but the first time you attempt it, talk to someone you trust, such as a banker or Independent Financial Adviser.

If you've been paying a home mortgage for several years, there is probably equity available from the payments you've made and rising values. The equity is the difference between the current appraised home value and what you owe on your mortgage. This can be borrowed as a home equity loan, also known as a second mortgage. Most lenders will loan up to 90 percent of the equity, and some even higher. I always like to borrow no more than 90 percent, which leaves a cushion should home values in the area fluctuate. I didn't want to have a house with a negative equity value. For most people, a home is the biggest investment they will make, so you want to be sure it's safe and secure.

Getting the loan is also easier because it's secured by property. A current appraisal is usually necessary to assure the lender of the exact value at the time of the loan. A reasonable credit score and regular income is about all you need in most cases. If your credit score is lower than the lender's target number, they may offer to lend a lower percentage of the equity, such as 75 or 80 percent. If you can't show a current salary, some lenders will accept *stated income* or monthly funds deposited in your current account. They just want to be sure you have the cash flow to repay the loan on time. It usually takes about two to three weeks from the start to when you receive your money, and there will be a closing meeting just like when you purchased your home the first time. A lot of documents will have to be signed, but they are mostly routine if you are dealing with a reputable source.

If you have a first mortgage at a higher interest rate than is currently available, you could consider refinancing before you go to a second home equity mortgage. You can refinance at a higher base amount than you currently owe and take the difference back payable to you. This money is yours to do with as you please, and can help a growing business or one that is in need of immediate cash. This also leaves the option open down the road for a home equity loan if values rise or more equity builds up. By doing it this way you will only have one monthly payment, but it will be larger.

There are probably other types of home equity loans and lenders that are always trying to be creative with new ideas. It's certainly a lot less hassle than going to a bank or applying for an unsecured loan. And if you're really afraid to put your house on the line for your business, maybe you're in the wrong business and you need a change. Or maybe small business is a bigger risk than you want to take—it's not for everyone. But if you love small business the way I do, check out the home equity loans. They can really help solve some urgent cash-shortage situations.

Raising capital is always a challenge for any small business owner. When money is needed *now*, there might be a tendency to panic a little and grab at the first source that becomes available. But it's always better to look at all the options and select the best one for your needs and ability to repay. Picking the wrong one may help you now, but may cause you greater problems later. The best way to decide on a money source is to check them out before you need them.

CHAPTER 23

Tax Problems

Paying taxes is a necessary evil for any civilised republic. We all want the comfort of living in a nation where we are protected from our enemies, have electricity, running water, pollution controls, and schools to educate our children. Well, these things are paid for by taxes from all the businesses and hard-working citizens. This is something we all know, but occasionally need to be reminded of. Anyway, we don't really have a choice; we all have to pay our fair share of taxes, and avoiding them or getting behind will cause unwanted tax problems.

Most streetwise business owners are aware of the taxes that need to be paid, and they make the best effort to get them paid on time. But similar to any other expense, where do you turn when the money for taxes is not all there? You can plan and put the money aside, but sometimes, unintentionally, you fall short of the total amount due. For some reason, this seems to happen when you least expect it, and when your business has entered its slow period.

Keeping up with tax payments should be on every business owner's must-do list, but how high do you put it? Is it number one, number two, number three, or even number six on the list? Does it come after rent and suppliers' invoices? What about paying your employees and their benefits? What happens if you don't pay your electric or phone bill? Can you still operate your business? So how high on your list do you put taxes, so you won't incur heavy penalties and demand letters? I'm sorry to say I don't have a set answer because, well, there just isn't one.

Sure, everyone will tell you, "pay those taxes first", but they're not in the situation and don't feel other pressures.

If you budget your expenses correctly, you should have all the money you need to pay all your taxes. But a budget is usually based on a certain amount of incoming capital that's available to pay those expenses. And what do you do when that incoming capital or cash flow is short by 20 or 30 percent? Now you can't pay all those other bills and taxes on time as you were planning to. One or two of them have to get put off, or you have to make partial payments. Because the tax collector will act more slowly than some of the others in many cases, you move that bill down your list a little. However, your intention is to take care of it as quickly as you can.

When you have a lot of different taxes and other bills due, it's sort of like running in a five-mile race. You want to stay out in front, so the one you're most concerned about is the other runner that's closest behind you. There may also be another 30 people in the race who are a little farther back, and you have to stay ahead of them also if you want to be the winner. You put the rest of the pack in the back of your mind for the moment. While you are busy taking care of your closest nemesis, the rest of the pack is also gaining on you. More of your energy is depleted and now everyone is within striking distance. That's how unpaid taxes are; they keep getting closer until the pressure is on you to pay NOW! They will never go away, and never forgets the government that you owe them. And if you completely ignore them, the penalties and interest keep growing.

So how do you know which taxes are the most urgent and should be your first choice to pay? Let me state here that I am NOT an accountant or IFA, and I'm not offering any legal advice. I just want to cover some of the situations that I have been involved with throughout the last 30 years of running many small businesses. I remember it was always a good feeling when I knew I was 100 percent paid up on all my taxes. But there were also other times when I slipped a little behind and got stuck paying that wasteful penalty and interest. And every time I got caught up, I always vowed never to get behind again. My intentions were always to be conscientious, but the rest of the business didn't consistently co-operate, so I would occasionally slip a little behind again and have to suffer another penalty.

Taxes are similar to any other expense in your business and they must be accounted for and paid if you want to keep operating. HM

Revenue & Customs has enforcement personnel that come into play when the written and mailed warnings are not adhered to. You always want to settle any overdue taxes before you get to that point if you possibly can. You want to avoid the tax collection officers from stopping in at your business or phoning you. But if it ever gets to that point, speak to them in a professional manner and explain your situation and why you got behind. They don't want to close your business, or put a levy on you unless you give them no other choice. Their job is to collect overdue taxes and keep you current in the future. So don't run and hide, dodge their calls, or slip away in the night. Meet the situation head-on, and come up with a solution you both can live with.

Tax collectors or enforcement officers are ordinary people like the rest of us. They have families, mortgage payments, credit card bills, and taxes similar to everyone else. They are trained to do their job and have no personal feeling for or against the delinquent taxpayer. They must follow procedures and make their best effort to collect any owed taxes. They are not always the most popular people you will meet in the course of your business, but they must be dealt with if the circumstances warrant it. And if you work with them to find a way you can satisfy what is owed, a plan can usually be agreed upon. It's just another one of those aggravating problems that most business owners like to sweep under the rug, but can't.

Payroll Taxes

This is one area that can be the easiest to get behind in because you, the business owner, control the payments or deposits. Because no one is looking over your shoulder on a daily basis, you have command of these funds. But just because there is no one monitoring you on a daily basis doesn't mean you're not being watched and checked on. The government has made you the custodian of these taxes (whether you like it or not), and trust you to deposit or send them in. If you betray that trust, you will get penalties, interest, and anything else they can find to throw at you. But believe it or not, you are supposed to know all of this by just being in business and having employees. It's sort of like a mother telling a 10-year-old to watch a big bowl of sweets on Halloween. You can give it out to people you don't know, but don't eat any yourself. The temptation is there and has to be dealt with sensibly.

So what are these taxes that get some small business owners in hot water if not paid on time? Here's a brief description:

- *Income Tax*—PAYE (Pay as you Earn) income tax must be deducted from all your employees' wages at source by you and sent to HM Revenue & Customs Income tax covers all earnings including benefits such as: company cars or vans, fuel for a vehicle, medical insurance, living accommodation or low-interest loans. Each employee has a tax-free allowance which entitles them to earn up to a certain sum (£5,435 in 2008-2009) before they begin to pay tax.

- *National Insurance*—In addition to Income Tax, each employee must pay National Insurance Contributions, which again must be deducted by you at source. NICs build up entitlement to certain social security allowances, including the state pension. The amount of contributions that your employees must pay depends on the level of their earnings. As an employer, you are also required to make a National Insurance Contribution for each of your employees.

It is your responsibility to set up and process these taxes for all the staff on your payroll. Full details of how to administer the payroll taxes in the UK are available from the HM Revenue & Customs website (www.hmrc.gov.uk).

If you don't fancy handling the process of paying your staff and deducting taxes yourself, there are good payroll services available that will actually do your entire payroll, including figuring deductions, printing wage slips, delivering them, and keeping track of the amounts you need to deposit or pay in. You will usually call, fax, or email the data to the payroll service, and they deliver your wage slips in two to three days.

Value Added Tax

Sure, we pay value added tax (VAT) on most of our purchases, but how does the government get it? We pay VAT to the merchant we are buying from, and never really see it again. Most consumers don't know where their VAT goes, and don't care. All they know is that it is added as a percentage to most purchases, so they pay it. Some items are exempt from VAT (zero-rated), some are taxed at the reduced rate of five per cent, but most are taxed at the standard rate of 17.5 per cent.

As a UK business owner you will have to register for VAT if your annual taxable turnover exceeds £61,000. You can still register for VAT if your turnover is less than this amount, but companies which exceed this limit and then fail to register for VAT face fines and other penalties. VAT exempt items which are excluded from your taxable turnover include training, insurance and loans.

To calculate the VAT you must pay as a business you need to work out the difference between the VAT you charge to your customers (output tax) and the VAT you pay to your suppliers (input tax). Deduct the input tax from the output tax and pay the balance to the Revenue. Again, you will find further information on VAT registration and exemption on the Revenue's website at www.hmrc.gov.uk.

Other Taxes

There are other taxes that you can get behind on or forget to file and pay. If you are the sole or part owner, or own stock in a closely held corporation, these can affect your operation. By knowing that all the different taxes can affect you, it will let you plan how to handle any that are overdue. Being surprised by not knowing will put you under more pressure when those final demand notices arrive. The more time you have to prepare or negotiate a payment plan in advance, the better you can figure out solutions. So be aware of all the different taxes that you are responsible for and decide how you will deal with them.

- *Corporation Tax*—This is a tax on profits paid only by limited companies. The self employed are not required to pay corporation tax, but the following types of organisation are NOT exempt: Trade and housing associations, members clubs and associations, certain types of collective group, such as co-operatives. There are different thresholds of corporation tax, depending on your level of profit.

- *Taxes for specific products, services and activities*— Depending on your particular area of business, you may find that there is an additional tax payable relating to your product or service. Common additional taxes include road fuel duty, insurance premium tax, gambling duties and air passenger duties.

- *Environmental taxes*—These are designed to encourage responsible use of the environment by businesses whose activities can be seen to have an impact on the environment around them. Environment taxes include an aggregates levy on sand gravel and rock extracted from the earth or sea bed around the coast, the climate change levy, which is a tax on commercial energy consumption and the landfill tax, which is a tax on those companies which dispose of waste at a landfill site.

- *Business rates*—Anyone who uses a building for non-domestic purposes is liable to pay business rates on that property. This is a local tax which aims to cover the cost of providing local authority services such as police and fire fighters. Each property has a rateable value, which is a calculation based on location plus a national government-set adjustment.

More information on all these taxes, allowances and rebates can be obtained from the Business Link website at www.businesslink.gov.uk.

Getting behind on payment or not filing a tax return can eventually affect your business. If the Revenue puts a levy on you and your property, they can also go after any business assets you have; that's why ignoring the notices that are posted to you will only get you more problems. If you respond or contact them, it usually buys a little more time for you to come up with a solution. But in most cases, you can set up a payment arrangement that will stop the notices, phone calls, or personal visits as long as you keep your promises. During a payment plan the penalties will stop, but the continual interest will not.

The Bottom Line

The bottom line is, you'll have to report and pay all your taxes eventually. There is no sure-fire escape if you want to be a UK citizen and live in the country comfortably. The government doesn't really care how or why you can't pay what's due; they just want payment as soon as possible. The tax collectors are doing the job they are paid to do and use or follow all the rules and laws available to them. Their intention is not to close down your business if there is any way they can collect the tax. They will try to work within your means on payment plans, but don't expect them to make it too easy. You must make a serious effort to negotiate the best plan you can.

And if you end up having your business closed or close it yourself, some of the taxes still won't go away. I can tell you almost for sure that any payroll taxes that were deducted from your employees' wages must be paid, whether you are still in business or not. The officer of the company that has access and signs on the payroll account is usually personally responsible for these taxes. If they can be paid in full by the officer, a payment plan will be set up for as long as it takes. It's wise not to let these taxes get too far behind because there is no escaping them later.

It all comes down to the fact that you *will* have to eventually pay all the different taxes that are due. Some are more critical than others, but they will likely never let you escape from them completely. So if you run into a situation in which you are going to get behind, don't let it go too far. When you get notices, respond by the due date listed even if you can't pay all the taxes that are due. I have sent partial payments and bought a little more time in some cases. Remember that the agency's job is to collect the tax first rather than levy or close you down. Don't forget to be courteous and businesslike to Revenue personnel; it could make a difference on a future decision.

CHAPTER 24

When There's No Hope Left

As we travel along the small business road, we encounter a lot of hills, valleys, and roadblocks. Most of the time, we are happy just to be on our own, and we love to achieve our goals and face all the challenges. Other times, we wonder why we ever started our business and feel as though we need a way to escape.

Maybe it all goes back to that risk-reward equation that many of us just can't pass up. We get this internal drive that keeps gnawing at us until we decide to play it out. The smartest will have a plan and plenty of resources going in, but others will just wing it without a lot of preparation. Some of us just make up our plan along the way with adjustments as they are needed. Although money is a great consideration, it wasn't why we went into business in the first place. We knew that if we made our business successful, financial rewards would automatically be there and we wouldn't have to chase money. Our goal was to build a great business and take the credit for the right decisions. But if it wasn't great, we were also ready to accept that responsibility, too.

I have seen businesses that became big quickly, and others that ceased to exist in a very short time. It's hard to say why some businesses close so quickly, but a lot of it can be traced back to how the owner was thinking as he or she went into it initially. If there was no plan, no goals, no invested learning time, and the owner was under-capitalised going in, there was probably less than a 50 percent chance of succeeding. That doesn't mean the business wouldn't or couldn't make it, it just means that the owner didn't use the tools to raise those odds. It's sort of like blackjack; you'll win sometimes, but the house always has the edge in the long run.

I hate to see a business that has to close or sell out at a fraction of what was invested. I know all the hard work that was put into it to make it successful, and in many cases, long hours. It's not even about the money, which is also gone. It's the dream that the entrepreneur had that has now turned into a nightmare. But it's also not the end of the world either; it's only business. Many of the great wealthy people today had one or more failures along their climb to prosperity. I guess, in some cases, it's knowing when to let go and pursue other avenues. It's okay to operate day to day for a little while, but you must see some longer term survival or goal that is reachable. The streetwise owner will know when it's time to throw in the towel because the fight can never be won. There is no textbook or college course that tells you when that time has come, you just have to be there and experience it.

But just as this chapter takes you into the depressing side of business, the last chapter is a new dawn. How quickly or soon the new sun rises depends on how well you handle the problems you are now facing. This is why it's so important to close and exit a business correctly and legally. Just locking the door, moving to another city, and changing your name won't do it. Let's remember when your business was doing well, you made many contacts and learned much about how a business really works. You can now use all that information in any future endeavours. I heard once that entrepreneurs that have gone out of business are usually back at their peak in a new venture within four to five years. If you're not already 90 years old, you have the time, so don't waste it. If at first you don't succeed…

Why Can't You Make It?

Declining Sales

This may have been going on for a long time, and you either didn't pay attention or you just ignored it. You tried to increase business with the same old methods that always worked before, but somehow they aren't doing as well now. Rather than find new marketing ideas, you figured that you would just sit it out and see what happened. You may have had plenty of customers, but they are also declining and not being replaced. Fixed expenses may be slowly increasing, but the sales that create the profits to pay them are not. As time goes on, the distance between expenses and profits gets wider in a negative direction. And because you let it go on too long, there is little money left to generate new marketing ideas to increase sales. If you can't quickly turn around sales, you have to seriously do some big downsizing or make the decision to close the business. And cutting prices, which reduces profits, will not solve the problem this time. Lower prices won't save you when sales are not increasing at the same time.

Industry or Product Changes

If this caught you off guard, you weren't doing your required homework and staying up to date on your industry. Big changes in products and services don't usually happen overnight; you see or hear some advance evidence of it coming. You may have been doing well with what you are selling and just ignored the talk and gossip about what new progress may be coming. Even the hot products of past times have gone by the wayside because of new innovations. How many people do you know that are still using tyres with tubes, flash cubes on their cameras, or cassettes? These were all hot products in their time, but were eventually replaced. Not much in this world lasts forever, not even us. This is why it is so important to attend your industry's trade shows, so if you waited too long and you just can't catch up at this stage in the game, you need to decide if you still want to stay in this business. You may want to even survey your customers and find out what they are going to do now that new products are available in the marketplace. Don't just guess, ask them.

Market Changes

This can happen to any market throughout time, but you should see it coming. If you build a business on a fad (short-lived) and it disappears like the pet rock or hula hoop, you better have another idea quick. Fads come and go quickly, and it's dangerous to make a big investment of time and money in something that could be gone tomorrow. A trend (longer than a fad) will give you more time to build your business and make profits, but that usually won't last permanently either. People seem to change their way of thinking over time, especially as new generations come into play. The types of markets that were popular in the 1980s changed in the 1990s, and may be

235

nonexistent in the 2000s. If you didn't change with them, you may be close to nonexistent in your business also. Never ignore a new product or innovation without first investigating its potential.

Uncontrollable Situations

Because they are almost impossible to predict (see Chapter 21), they can catch you off guard and leave you in a hopeless situation. What do you do if you have a long-standing family restaurant, which caters to travellers and tourists, when the main road to you is cut off? The new motorway is going over you and the nearest exit will be more than a mile away. If you don't figure out another source of customers to fill those empty tables, you may have to admit defeat. You can get all the petitions signed that you want, but you probably won't be able to stop the road. What's that old saying, "You can't beat the government"? Some businesses can come back from weather disasters and some can't; each circumstance is different. Another situation you can't control is when a supplier that provides you with a unique product closes down, or if the owner of this business dies and the heirs decide to liquidate. If it's a mainstay of your business and it comes as a surprise, you could also be in jeopardy. When there are no other sources of supply, this could be devastating if it catches you off guard. That's why I always suggest having backup supply sources.

How to Get Out Gracefully

When you know for sure that you are not going to continue in your business, you will have to decide how you're going to close it. If you just run away and hide, you will have little or no chance of ever trying again in the future. Creditors and the Revenue will find you eventually, and then you'll have worse problems and bigger amounts that you will have to settle or be responsible for. It's not that difficult to close a business correctly, and it will save you many headaches in the future, so choose a way that will leave you free and clear to go on to something else. You don't want problems and aggravation coming back to haunt you months and years later. Get it over with, do it right, and get a clean start without looking over your shoulder all the time. Depending on your current situation, there are a few choices that will be best for you.

Sell Off to a Larger Company

If your business is in trouble financially, you won't look too attractive as a purchase candidate unless you have some valuable assets. Used furniture and equipment are not worth very much and won't bring more than 10 or 15p in the pound unless it's very unique or custom made, and even then not much more. Possibly your most valuable assets may be intangible; these are your customers and mailing lists. Because they can no longer purchase from you, why not recommend another company for them to contact? This could be worth much more than any equipment or office furniture to an interested buyer. Get together and write a letter to all major accounts or customers telling them that after you close, you recommend they now purchase from... You can actually sign the letter and put it on your letterhead. If you don't have the money for printing and postage, make the cost something the buying company pays for. If the products or services are somewhat unique, the new company can expect 50- to 80-percent response from this mailing. It should also receive all the repeat orders if it services the customers as well as you did. You could also include some of your own time to help with the transition. So if this is an option, check out who your biggest competitors are and be ready to contact them. This needs to be done *before* you cut off sales to customers.

Close on Your Own

This is the most desirable way, but most businesses may not be able to do it financially. You should have almost all the money you need to pay most of your open bills and just be able to walk away. If you are closing because you're tired of the business and would be unable to sell it, this is an option you can actually consider. If you pay all your utility bills, loans and taxes, then all you should have left is suppliers and expenses. If you don't quite have 100 percent of the money needed to pay all these in full, you can try to offer a reasonable payoff. Compose a letter that explains that you are closing your business and address it to all the creditors you still owe. Advise them that although you would prefer to pay them in full, your limited resources won't let you. Make an offer of 80 to 90 percent of what you owe to be paid immediately upon receiving a signed release from them. Anyone you owe a larger amount to should receive a registered letter, so you are sure that it gets there. I don't think an offer of lower than 80 percent is going to work in all cases, and you might end up in a few lawsuits. Your objective is to walk away free and clear, and all obligations are finalised. But you'll never know for sure if they will accept your offer unless you ask.

The Insolvent Business

Insolvency occurs when a business can no longer pay its debts because there is not enough money in its accounts or within its assets.

Unlike other parts of Europe and the USA, in the UK, businesses cannot go bankrupt, they can only go into liquidation. Here, the term bankruptcy is reserved only for personal circumstances and not businesses. The effect is much the same, but the procedures and terms of reference are different from country to country.

Some people think of liquidation as their first and only choice, but really it's the last. As you have seen throughout this book, there are many ways to solve a lot of the problems before it even gets this far. But if you feel that the debt pressure is just too great and there is no way to get out from under in the near term, then liquidation may be the next step. For purposes of this book, we are only going to briefly go over the business situation, not personal bankruptcy, and a good lawyer who specialises in the business part can save you a lot of time and headaches. Most of them will want a retainer in advance, for obvious reasons. Good legal advice is important to be sure you don't miss any steps, and follow the laws exactly. Here's a quick guide to some of the key avenues open to you in this situation:

Administration and CVA

When an insolvent company goes into administration using a court ordered Administration Order, a court appointed official will reorganise the company in an attempt to make it profitable again. A Company Voluntary Arrangement (CVA) is a similar process which allows the management of the company to remain in place while attempting to sort out the financial problems. A CVA is normally agreed at a formal meeting of a company's creditors. The plan must win the support of at least 75 per cent of the creditors to go ahead.

Receivership

Banks which have lent money to a UK business on a secured basis have the right to call in a receiver to reorganise the assets of a company and protect the bank's assets. This is sometimes a precursor to winding up, but sometimes a company in receivership can recover.

Liquidation

This is really the point of no return. When a company goes into voluntary liquidation, or is wound up by a court, it stops all operations and goes completely out of business. It will almost certainly never be reformed. At this stage a liquidator is appointed to sell off the company's remaining assets and the money generated by this sale is then used to pay off any outstanding debts. It is highly unlikely that all creditors will see their money again, as there is a strict pecking order of creditor repayment, beginning with tax authorities, then banks with secured loans and then other creditors such as unsecured loan lenders, suppliers and (normally last of all) employees.

Negotiate Out of Court

This is similar to entering a CVA, but there is no need to go to court. You need to hire an experienced business lawyer to be your organiser. He will be on your side all the way, but also looking out for creditors. Usually a letter is sent to your biggest creditors asking them to attend a meeting at your lawyer's office. The lawyer will explain your situation, with you in attendance, and try to work out a plan so your business can continue operating. Most creditors will want to see that you stay open, so they can recover what you owe them. They probably already know you're having problems if you are behind on your payments to them. Your lawyer will do most of the talking, but you should be there to show that you are sincere in making any plan work.

Once they accept your reorganisation plan or make revisions that you concur with, they should all sign some sort of agreement. The plan should start immediately, and your lawyer will compose a letter to all your other creditors explaining what has been agreed upon to keep you operating. There is no automatic stay to stop the collection calls, but your creditors can be referred to your lawyer's office for further information. Most other smaller creditors will accept the plan, but there may be one or more who don't. This type of reorganisation is best if you can do it, because the fees are smaller and it gives you more freedom.

CHAPTER 25

Starting Over Again

When you have to close your business, what are you going to do next? Is it time to give up the small business idea and go back to work for another company? If you're not ready to retire yet, a decision has to be made, but this decision should not be made too quickly. Try to take at least a week or two off after the dust has settled from your last venture; you don't want to go into a new business with any leftover stress from the last one. But the real question you have to ask is whether you really want to do it again. Remember that anyone can open a business, but it takes a lot more effort to operate it. And if you've been through it once before, you know the effort it will take; there are few, if any, shortcuts to success.

If your decision is to go ahead, the first thing I would suggest is to write down all the reasons why you weren't successful in your previous business(es). Don't just think about it, write it down so you see it, and can refer back to it in the future. What streetwise lessons have you learned, and how will that help you in any tough times ahead? You want to be aware of any mistakes that you made and avoid them in any new business. If you don't, you might be right back in the same situation five years from now, so do it right this time and build a company that will last and you can be proud of. You need to revive that drive and perseverance that you had in the past.

If you closed a business and are opening a similar one within six months, don't make it look anything like the previous one. If some creditors weren't paid in full or not paid at all, they could open an investigation about fraud in closing the old business. Keep good records of everything, especially if you purchased any furniture or equipment for the old business that you will be using in the new company. Don't use a name that sounds similar to the old one. Make it completely different and register it as a new business. This is a fresh start with a new company, and it has to look and act that way. No one should be able to connect the two in any way.

You need to decide whether you will be starting the same kind of business that you just closed or a completely different one. If it's going to be similar to the last one, you may want to make some adjustments this time. Go over which products or services made you the most profits and which ones didn't; then decide if your new business can eliminate some of the low profit ones. In some cases, you might not be able to get rid of some of them because they complement the others. For example, if you make good profits selling exhausts but only break even on the installation of them, why not stop installing them? You really can't, because who is going to buy an exhaust from you and then try to find someone else to put it on their car? It's better in a case like this to figure out how to increase profitably on the service end because you can't operate your business without it.

Next you need to decide if your last customer base was profitable. Did you try to target a market area that was too big or too small? Were some of your customers more trouble than they were worth in profit? Can you expand or narrow your target market now and be more profitable? Think of past customers and decide which 10 percent you would not like to sell to in the future. Remember, you only want to have customers you can serve well and make a fair profit on.

Going to school on what did or did not make your previous business successful is the classic streetwise way. There is no other way to learn it other than being there day after day right in the middle of your business. You got the chance firsthand to see your ideas in progress and how they turned out. Even if many of them didn't work out, you now know, and you have a fresh start with new ideas. After years of experiments trying to invent the light bulb, someone asked Thomas Edison if he knew how a light really worked. He said, "Not yet, but I know thousands of ways that it doesn't work." Always an optimist, he finally found the answer, and the rest, as they say, is history. Sometimes trial and error is the only way to find out.

Although you may not have many years and thousands of chances to prove your success, you can learn from past experiences. That's why the short time between closing one business and opening another can be used to analyse past results. If you're not exactly sure where you went off track before, ask your previous employees, suppliers, or your accountant. They will all have some opinion if you're really willing to listen to them. Because your old employees are no longer under your command, they may speak more freely, and you could really learn something. Don't pass up this chance to learn some valuable lessons.

If you are going into a different type of business than the one you just exited, you can still apply some of the lessons and principles. Many small businesses can be operated in a similar manner; just the products and services are different. The basics of the business are the same: cash flow, payroll, taxes, payables, and so on, so previous experience can always be used and errors made in the past can now be corrected. Read books in the areas you feel you have weaknesses. Take a computer class at a local college if you need more knowledge in how to use them in your business.

The New Plan

Before you jump into a new business with both feet, try creating a plan this time. You can call it your business plan or whatever, but it should be a written direction for your new endeavour. If you're the only one who will look at it, neatness is not important as long as you can refer back to it often and understand it. If you are going to submit it to a lender, then neatness does count. There are many books in stores and libraries about how to develop a business plan, and you should refer to them. If you feel you're not very good at writing one, contact a local secretarial or business service company to help you. After you explain what you want in it, they will put it into words for you. It's worth the extra money to have it professionally done for any important presentations. It will create a good first impression with any lenders, major suppliers, or even relatives if you are looking for an investment.

Your plan should be goal-oriented; realistic goals and reasonable time periods to reach them are the best. Saying that your sweetshop is going to reach £2million in sales within two years is a bit far-fetched. Who's going to believe it, especially if your start up capital is only £20,000? If you want people to accept your plan and help you be more pragmatic, certainly be optimistic and sell your plan—just don't go overboard. And I hate the word *try* in any business plan—don't use it. *Try* is for losers, and you want to be a winner. You aren't going to *try* to be a success; you are going to *be* a success. And if you don't believe it, why should anyone else? Would you loan any money to someone who said they would *try* to pay it back?

If you're not going to submit your business plan to lenders or anyone else, consider making an outline of the steps to your goals. I prefer an outline because it's easy to read quickly, and it reminds you of actions you want to take. I always write a brief outline for each chapter in my books so I don't forget areas I want to cover as I'm writing it. Sometimes ideas come quickly, and if you don't list them in an outline, you might not remember them later. And don't create an outline of things you plan to do and then misplace it. Make a copy and keep one at your business and one at home. Hang it on the wall where you can easily see it.

The Franchise Option

You do have another choice in starting a new business. If you are sure you want a small business, but are not sure you want to come up with all the answers yourself, think about a franchise. There are so many different franchises out there that one should be available in your area of interest. In fact, there should be more than one, so you can compare and select the one you feel most comfortable with. In my other book, *Chasing Success: A Street Smart Guide to Owning a Business*, there is an entire chapter dedicated to starting a franchise and what to look for. Once you write the cheque for the franchise fee and you are accepted by the management, there's no turning back. You must do your due diligence well in advance and get all your questions answered to your satisfaction. Rarely, if ever, is the initial fee you paid refundable, and it could be thousands of pounds. So if they are giving you too much pressure to sign and pay, back off and really think it through. At the very least, talk to other franchisees and get the real facts. Don't be too quick to jump in with both feet (and your wallet)—investigate, investigate, investigate.

A franchise that you are comfortable with can take a lot of difficult decisions off your mind, because the franchise company has probably already made them in the past. Its representatives can advise you about what will and won't work, because they feel they have a proven plan for success. Although there is never a guarantee that you will make a profit, the chance may be better than going it alone. But you must follow their plan and agree to run your business according to it. Big national franchise chains will be more strict and will have representatives checking on you regularly to make sure you are following their rules. You will pay a royalty (a percent of gross sales) and possibly an additional fee to be used for advertising. Smaller franchise chains may not do as much advertising, but will supply in-store signs and displays.

But similar to any other business, you are still responsible for your own domain. If it doesn't succeed, you can't go running back to the franchise office with "but, but, but." You might even want to do some of your own advertising and promotion in your local target market. You will probably need some sort of prior approval from the main office before you spend those pound. The people there will want to see that you are following the image they have built. It shouldn't be too difficult to get their go-ahead if your plan fits their standards and corporate goals. After all, they want you to increase sales because they are getting a percentage of it.

Another advantage of a franchise is that all your suppliers will already be set, and there may even be a corporate discount that all franchises get. Your supply and ordering procedures will be easier than going it alone, but if you find a new local source of supply, it may be hard to get the okay to use it because of contracts with others. You must follow the rules you agreed to when you signed your franchise agreement. Sure, you have less freedom, but you also have a plan and a franchise office that wants to help you succeed. Many franchises have opened several stores and offices and grown quite large. Just be sure it's in an industry that you enjoy, and that you can handle the hours required.

Re-establishing Credit

If you recently closed a business, there could be some future credit problems. If it was a corporation or LLP, your personal credit should not be affected at all. But many industries have credit groups with a huge membership, and submit data on problem customers. When you go out of business in the printing industry, for example, your past company name and the names of owners or officers get put into a database, so if you start another company or distributorship and contact different suppliers, they will have access to that information if they are members of that credit group. So you can't just close down on one street and open next week on another and think no one will notice. When you closed your previous business, there were probably many suppliers who took losses, and you can't always escape them with these credit groups.

If you are questioned about your past business, never lie, but don't go into too much depth, either. Explain that you now have a completely new company that has no association at all with the last one. You don't feel there will be any problems paying on time; ask how you can establish credit with them. They will probably require full or partial payment on the first few orders and will gradually increase your credit limit as you go along. Of course, they will be watching closely how you pay balances due in the beginning. Most suppliers will want your orders if you can convince them you will pay on time. You could offer to give them a personal guarantee on the first few orders; that makes you responsible to pay if your company doesn't. But I would have something in writing that says the guarantee is cancelled after 60 or 90 days (or a certain number of orders). You don't want a personal guarantee to come up five years later when you have forgotten about it.

You will also get offers in the mail for company credit cards, which are always good to have. Most of the approval for these will come from checking the personal credit of the owners or officers. You can also apply for these online at most credit card company websites. Be sure to look for the application that specifies business credit cards, and always check out the interest rate, annual fee, and other costs. There should be several companies that you can choose from, so compare interest rates carefully. Don't be lured by a low rate as an introductory offer that goes sky high later. Other things to check are the grace period, any balance transfer fee, and charges for over-the-limit and late payments.

You will want to open a new current account for your new business right away. I would suggest that you use a different bank than you used before. Bankers and loan officers are like elephants—they never forget. Many banks now offer some type of credit that's tied to your current account and covers any overdrafts. You can also use it to borrow small amounts as needed, but you aren't likely to get any credit at the previous bank that knew you closed a business. This also is based on the owner's personal credit and any previous business information they know of. And if you're using some of the same suppliers, you don't want any cheques to look like those of your old company. If you're making a fresh start, be sure everything looks that way.

If you want to establish credit as a new company, don't go into it on a shoestring and be under financial pressure right from the start. If you don't think you have enough start-up capital, wait until you get more. Review the ideas in Chapter 22 or come up with other plans. Be prepared and willing to pay suppliers up front for the first few orders so you can create that comfort zone. Any hesitation on prepayment in the beginning will make credit departments wonder if you're already having money problems on the first orders. They might back off and make it even more difficult to establish credit, especially if they lost any money on you from the previous company. Don't plead or beg, just be professional.

Be Prepared

If you love small business as much as I do, then you want everyone to succeed. I don't care if it is a competitor of mine or not, there should be enough business out there for all of us. And if there isn't, let's get together and steal it from the big companies. Small business has been and will be the innovators of new products and services in this country. We have also created more new jobs while the big corporations are cutting their staff. Even the government is beginning to realise how important small business is to a healthy economy. So before you give in and take that salaried job in a big company, weigh up your decision carefully. Remember, if you've been through it already, you're smarter now, and that will give you an advantage.

But once you have made the decision to start another business, be prepared going into it. As I said earlier, you learned many lessons the last time around; use them to get off on the right foot this time. You should be smarter this time and know the ways that will and won't succeed. Maybe what you took for granted came back to haunt you later; now you know. Have some type of a goal, on paper, of what you are going to do and how you are going to do it. Here are a few things you will want to consider before you start:

- What industry will you be in?
- What is your source of start-up capital?
- What is your source of additional capital if needed?
- Will you be the same or different type of business?
- Will you be franchise or be independent?
- Where it will be located?
- What are your marketing plans?
- What suppliers will you need?
- What bank will you use?
- What furniture and equipment will you need?
- How will you get customers?
- Will you have a website?
- Who will do your bookkeeping?
- When will your first day be?
- Will you need employees right away?
- Are you mentally ready?

By having a plan and goal, you will be giving yourself a better chance for success this time. Have others who may be working with you review your plan and give suggestions. The fewer surprises that pop up after you start, the better. You want to concentrate on building your new business rather than scramble around doing things you forgot. Keep an open and clear mind going in and realise that there will be some problems that arise. But you should be wiser this time and be able to solve them more quickly. Problems happen to everyone. Just keep chipping away at success and remember that a mansion can't be built in a week. Start with a good foundation and work your way up. Success is out there waiting for you, so go for it!

Index

About The Author

Barry Thomsen started his entrepreneurial career when he was only 5 years old. He decided that he wasn't going to sit for hours in front of his house and try to sell a pitcher of lemonade, so he loaded two pitchers in his wagon and took them to nearby construction sites; he sold out in 15 minutes. Meanwhile, his friends' pitchers were still almost full. At age 10, he was given the worst paper round because he was the youngest, but he tripled the number of subscribers within a year.

Growing up on the southwest side of Chicago automatically made him streetwise. To make extra money when he first got married, he sold Amway, Avon, and a family portrait programme door to door. By working on his own, he learned firsthand the importance of great customer service. Then working on commission at a computer placement service, he became the number-two producer out of 40 people. To learn other types of businesses, he also worked part-time as a bartender at a bowling centre, delivered pizzas, and rose to assistant manager at a chain pizza store. Next, he worked evenings and weekends at a family-owned Italian restaurant where he learned food service and how to handle slow and busy periods.

Now he was ready to take the plunge and try his hand at a business of his own—well, almost. With another associate from the placement service, he opened an employment agency as a partnership. After a year or so, Barry wanted more, so he started a computer supplies distributorship at the same time. After building extensive mailing lists for both companies, he sold these to other non-competitors and did very well with three businesses going at the same time.

As time went on and interests changed, he became an expert in old collector cookie jars, the rare ones being worth hundreds of dollars each. He started buying and selling them nationwide by direct mail (there was no eBay then). Next, he started a business-forms company in the mid-1980s, which grew to more than 3 million in sales after 14 years. During those years, he also became a collector and seller of old rare casino chips and authentic hand-signed Norman Rockwell lithographs. He bought and sold enough of these to purchase a second home in Colorado, where he now lives.

As more years passed and he gained more knowledge, he became a partner in a retail ice cream store and sold decorative Oriental items at an antique mall. Then he started his current business, which sells plastic cards and promotional items. During those years, he advised and helped many other small business people with start-up and other ideas to grow. He found he got a lot of personal satisfaction from helping others, so he started a monthly newsletter called the *Idea-Letter*, which has subscribers nationwide. He started writing small business articles, many of which are published in magazines, newspapers, and on the AMA website.

Barry decided to write a book to share all the good and bad experiences he has encountered along the way. He knew that the life of a small business person was not all fun and profits, but sometimes problems and even disasters. He loves small business, and even though the road has been rocky at times, he wouldn't have it any other way.

Barry Thomsen is also the publisher and editor of a monthly small business marketing newsletter called the *Idea-Letter*. For a free sample issue and subscription information, email idealetter@aol.com.

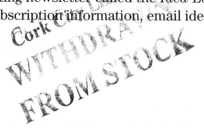

Barry Thomsen is also the publisher and editor of a monthly small business marketing newsletter called the *Idea-Letter*. For a free sample issue and subscription information, email idealetter@aol.com.